Praise for *Seeing Red*

…I can't express enough how much I love this book. [It] really focuses on
what is behind the anger, how you have power over your reaction to angry
feelings, and ways to cope with that anger. It is very engaging and fun!

—Danielle Schultz, author, School Counselor Blog www.schcounselor.com

Seeing Red is an excellent resource for anyone working with children who
need help self-regulating their emotions. As a busy professional, it is often
difficult to find the time to create lessons and do the planning necessary to
run quality groups. Jennifer Simmonds has done the work for you! You can
open up the *Seeing Red* curriculum and follow it each week with confidence.
The kids grow from the quality experiences and practice they get from
participating in the program. The lessons are creative and will hold their
attention while providing real skill building. This resource should be in
everyone's professional tool box! I wouldn't dream of doing my job without it.

—Lisa Hansen, school counselor

Seeing Red offers a roadmap for steering our children through the scary and
misunderstood feelings of anger. Clear lesson plans, clues for the leader, and
a simple supply list make this curriculum accessible for even the busiest
school social worker or group facilitator. Jennifer Simmonds has provided an
invaluable curriculum for teaching angry kids how to hold onto their best
selves during times of stress and emotional dysregulation.

—Chris Dooley-Harrington, LICSW, Children's Grief Specialist

We teach kids important skills like reading and writing so they can get along
in the world. We also need to teach kids the key skills needed to get along with
other people. Anger management is one of those crucial skills and *Seeing Red*
is a wonderful step by step program to teach children how to do it.

—David Walsh, PH.D., President, National Institute on Media and the Family

The *Seeing Red* curriculum has been helpful for my students, enabling them to think about specific situations, to break them down, and to recreate new ways of handling their anger. Students have an opportunity to learn that everyone gets angry and that it is a normal feeling. This curriculum helps them understand different and more positive ways of expressing their anger.

—Leslie Colerin, School Social Worker, Anne Sullivan Communication Center

The *Seeing Red* curriculum is very well laid out for the facilitator. It offers interactive activities to bring about discussion on a very serious topic, and does so in a fun and effective manner. Each lesson builds upon the others, creating a comprehensive and thorough curriculum that fosters learning and an understanding of anger as an emotion, and that it is how we deal with anger that makes a difference.

—Julie Neitzel Carr, Resolution and Prevention Program, YWCA of Minneapolis

Seeing Red

Seeing Red

an anger management and
anti-bullying curriculum for kids

Jennifer Simmonds

new society
PUBLISHERS

Cover design by Diane McIntosh.
Illustration by Lydia English.

Printed in Canada. First printing April 2014.

New Society Publishers acknowledges the financial support of the Government of Canada
through the Canada Book Fund (CBF) for our publishing activities.

Paperback ISBN: 978-0-86571-760-2 eISBN: 978-1-55092-564-7

Inquiries regarding requests to reprint all or part of *Seeing Red*
should be addressed to New Society Publishers at the address below.

To order directly from the publishers, please call toll-free (North America)
1-800-567-6772, or order online at www.newsociety.com

Any other inquiries can be directed by mail to:

New Society Publishers
P.O. Box 189, Gabriola Island, BC V0R 1X0, Canada (250) 247-9737

LIBRARY AND ARCHIVES CANADA CATALOGUING IN PUBLICATION

Simmonds, Jennifer, author

Seeing red : an anger management and anti-bullying curriculum for kids
/ Jennifer Simmonds. -- Revised and updated edition.

Revision of: Seeing red : an anger management and peacemaking curriculum for kids : a resource for teachers, social workers, and youth leaders / Jennifer Simmonds. – Gabriola, B.C. : New Society Publishers, 2003.

Includes bibliographical references.

Issued in print and electronic formats.

ISBN 978-0-86571-760-2 (pbk.).--ISBN 978-1-55092-564-7 (ebook)

1. Anger--Study and teaching (Elementary). 2. Anger--Prevention--Study and teaching (Elementary)--Activity
programs. 3. Conflict management Study and teaching (Elementary). 4. Interpersonal relations--Study and
teaching (Elementary). 5. Bullying--Study and teaching (Elementary). 6. Bullying--Prevention--Study and
teaching (Elementary)--Activity programs.

I. Title.

BF723.A4S55 2014   155.4'1247   C2014-901837-1
                                                             C2014-901838-X

New Society Publishers' mission is to publish books that contribute in fundamental ways to building an
ecologically sustainable and just society, and to do so with the least possible impact on the environment, in
a manner that models this vision. We are committed to doing this not just through education, but through
action. The interior pages of our bound books are printed on Forest Stewardship Council®-registered acid-
free paper that is 100% post-consumer recycled (100% old growth forest-free), processed chlorine-free, and
printed with vegetable-based, low-VOC inks, with covers produced using FSC®-registered stock. New Society
also works to reduce its carbon footprint, and purchases carbon offsets based on an annual audit to ensure a
carbon neutral footprint. For further information, or to browse our full list of books and purchase securely,
visit our website at: **www.newsociety.com**

Contents

Part 1: Introduction

Part 2: Sessions

PART 1

Introduction

All the worksheets in this book are available for download at

http://tinyurl.com/SeeingRedWorksheets

About *Seeing Red*

Anger is a natural human emotion, but if it isn't managed properly, its effects can be devastating. *Seeing Red* is a curriculum designed to help elementary and middle-school-aged students better understand their anger so they can make healthy and successful choices and build strong relationships. This completely revised and updated edition includes an anti-bullying component, specific to cyber-bullying and social media, as well as a strong focus on learning to self-regulate their behavior.

Designed especially for use with small groups, *Seeing Red* enables participants to learn from and empower one another. Its unique group process helps children and teens build important developmental objectives such as leadership skills (taking initiative, presenting in front of the group), social skills (taking turns, active listening), and building self-esteem (problem solving, interacting with peers).

Key concepts and activities include:

- Identifying anger triggers
- Taking responsibility for mistakes
- Finding healthy ways to deal with provocation and avoid losing control
- Stating feelings, learning steps to control anger, and exploring consequences
- Building their "tool box" with over a dozen strategies to self-regulate their feelings and behaviors

Facilitators will learn how to empower participants through role-playing; helping them to identify associated feelings and recognize negative behaviors.

Design and Framework of Lesson Plans

Key Principles of Seeing Red

Kids have the ability to...

1. Regulate and control their behavior

2. Problem solve together and make healthy choices

3. Be leaders and role models among their peers

4. Take responsibility for their behavior and choices

One of the key components throughout the *Seeing Red* sessions is helping kids learn to self-regulate their behavior. Self-regulation is not an isolated skill so kids must translate what they experience into information they can use to regulate their thoughts, emotions, and behaviors. Instead of impulsively pushing someone, for example, they can learn to say to themselves, "I'm not going to push her back," and then fold their arms. These skills develop gradually as they learn to identify their anger triggers, and think through the situation and demonstrate self-control. Everyone learns to self-regulate at a different pace, and it comes more easily for some than others, but it's a crucial life skill to learn. According to Ellen Galinsky, president and co-founder of the Families and Work Institute and author of *Mind in the Making*, regulating one's thinking, emotions, and behavior is critical for success in school, work, and life (2010).

Framework

- This curriculum is specifically designed for a small group (six to eight participants) of elementary or middle-school-aged children who are willing to participate in such a group.

- The ideal group should convene weekly in a confidential space with the same group members and facilitators attending each session.

- The curriculum is meant to be used in generally the same order because as the lessons progress, group members will build upon skills learned from previous sessions.

- Depending on the age and "personality" of your group, you can add, substitute, or leave out certain activities or sessions. For example, if you have a group of eight- and nine-year-olds, it may not be appropriate to focus on cyber-bullying and social media (but general bullying, yes!).

- Because not all strategies work for all kids, there are a variety of activeities described throughout the sessions. Customize specific needs and goals of your group.

In this order, each of the twelve sessions includes:

- Goals and objectives

- List of supplies needed for the various activities

- Description of tasks to be done prior to the start of the lesson

- Background notes to the leader about the general theme of the session

- Warm-up activity at the start of each meeting

- Thorough explanation of each learning activity

- Closing activity, and

- Tool box item to take home with them each week

Additions to the Newly Updated and Revised *Seeing Red*

The purpose of this updated and revised *Seeing Red* is to keep some of the "tried and true" themes and activities that have proven effective in helping kids manage their anger, but also offer new themes and new activities to use.

New themes included in the updated and revised *Seeing Red*:

- Building an internal tool box each session with a focus on a specific skill to either help them regulate their emotions strategies to making positive choices

- Explore the roles of the bully, victim, and bystander, with an emphasis on the powerful role the bystander plays in the dynamic

- Sessions focused on technology specific to cyberbullying and social media

- The importance of asking for forgiveness, as well as saying "I'm sorry"

- Teaching self-regulating calming techniques

- Weekly affirmations

- Supplemental ideas and learning activities to incorporate in your *Seeing Red* group

- Section on facilitating groups with kids and key elements of group process

- Additional list of books and resources

Important Notes

Tool Box

On the first week, participants will need a box that they bring home with them to serve as their "tool box." Each week following, there will be a tool box item that they bring home with them and put in their box to serve as reminders of the skill they have focused on during that particular week.

Scream Boxes

The Scream Box project in Session 9 requires materials that likely need to be collected over a period of time. Keep that in mind and plan ahead to have enough cereal boxes, paper towel rolls, and newspaper for everyone.

Supplemental Activities Section

If you need additional activities, or would like to incorporate specific routines as a part of your *Seeing Red* group, there are additional activities and ideas described starting on page 121.

Say to the group

There are instances in each session where it reads, "Say to the group…" There is not an expectation that you read those specific words, but it is offered as a guide for you as to the general message you want to be giving. Just be yourself and use words that are comfortable and natural to you.

Group Process

Benefits of Working With Kids in Groups

- Groups enable kids to form bonds with peers in a structured environment that enables them to discuss feelings and ideas openly.

- A group setting enables kids to understand that their feelings are not unique to them and that there is not something wrong with them. They can better appreciate others' experiences and gain perspective on their own lives.

- Through activities and discussions, they are able to articulate personal feelings and give feedback to their peers that would be more difficult to verbalize with adults. Kids often accept feedback better from peers than other adults.

- Group settings allow a program to reach more kids at one time.

- Social environment fulfills need for autonomy and identity.

A well-conceived use of program, what the group does together, can add texture to the group experience, fueling its capacity to transform itself into a unique entity, something new and special that has never existed before. Program is the unbreakable, malleable stuff that real-life groups are made of, creating "something-ness from "nothing-ness.

Andrew Malekoff
Group Work with Adolescents: Principles and Practice.
Second Edition. The Guilford Press, Inc. 2004

Tuckman Theory: The 5 Stages of Group Development

Dr. Bruce Tuckman published his group model in 1965. He added a fifth stage, Adjourning, in the 1970s. The Forming Storming Norming Performing theory is a helpful explanation of the group process, from when a group begins to when it ends. Tuckman's model explains that as the group develops and as relationships and roles are established, the facilitator leadership style shifts as well.

Stage 1: Forming

- Individual roles and responsibilities are unclear.

- Group members are looking for safe, patterned behavior.

- Group members are looking for guidance and direction so there is a high dependence on the facilitator.

- Group members are "checking everyone out," including the leaders, and making lots of judgments. There is usually little or no investment in the group yet.

Stage 2: Storming

- Group members are trying to figure out "their place" or role in the group.

- Competition and conflict arise, either covertly or overtly, as they assess and test the role of each group member and the facilitator. There is often a fear of exposure and rejection. Distrust.

- During this stage, the group has a strong need for structure and clarification. Seeks safety in boundaries.

- In order to progress to the next stage, group members must move from a "testing and proving" mentality to a problem-solving mentality.

- The most important trait in helping groups move is the ability to listen—validate experiences, exhibit strong boundaries, and be loyal in all aspects of the group.

Stage 3: Norming

- Roles and responsibilities are clear and accepted.

- Big decisions are made by group agreement.

- Smaller decisions may be delegated to individuals or small groups within the group.

- There is general respect for the leader and some of leadership is shared by the group.

- The group is cohesive and engaged.

- Group members are making contributions to the group. Group is "Productive"— working level and creativity are high.

- Level of trust is high.

Stage 4: Performing

(This stage is not reached by all groups. You can have a very healthy and productive group without moving into the Performing stage.)

- True interdependence.

- Can work independently, and there is complete equality between group members.

- Production level is very high.

- Loyalty is intense, and morale is high.

- Anxiety among group members can increase with the anticipation of the group ceasing.

Stage 5: Adjourning

- Adjourning is the breakup of the group, hopefully when the task has been completed successfully and its purpose achieved.

- Hopefully group members feel good about what's been accomplished, and therefore, recognition of their contribution should be acknowledged.

- Opportunity to say good-bye.

Keys to a Positive Group Process

- Establish group guidelines early on. Get input from everyone, and hold group members accountable for the guidelines they created.

- Believe the group can make good decisions on behalf of the group.

- Draw out quieter group members by asking them direct questions that are low risk, then thank them for their input.

- If a problem or issue arises in the group, turn the problem over to the group. (Example: "I'm noticing that the same people seem to be making most the decisions. How do you think we can be sure to get everyone's ideas heard?")

- Establish routines or rituals. Examples could include consistently begin with a check-in, an icebreaker, a sentence starter, or affirmation.

- Allow them to make decisions and have some say in what happens in the group so they feel ownership.

- Encourage the participants to communicate directly with one another instead of only through the facilitators. Whenever you have the opportunity, turn it over to the group: "What do you think about what Lisa said?"

- Empower the participants. Have different group members play some leadership roles each week, perhaps asking them if they have an activity/game to teach.

- Stay neutral and fair. Treat group members equally, allowing everyone the opportunity to lead, and to follow.

- Let them know that each person is valuable. Affirm and encourage the group. Take time to say, "Thanks for sharing that" or "What a neat idea!"

- Be aware of any confidentiality issues inside and outside the group. Although *Seeing Red* groups are not therapy groups, they may share some personal things that should not be shared outside of the group. It's important group members understand that "what's said in group, stays in group," with the exception of if you learn they are being harmed or want to harm themselves.

Facilitator Skills That Can Enhance the Group Process

Flexibility

The ability to fulfill different group roles at various times, such as: leader, supporter, inquisitor, "enforcer." This allows the group to fluidly move back and forth from "task" to "process." However, consistency in approach is important.

Confidence

To instill confidence in the group by appearing purposeful and in control, therefore calming group insecurities.

Authenticity

Be honest and be yourself.

Leadership (Presence)

To guide and influence the group through accurately listening, observing, and remembering.

Integrity

To be an example to the group of how to conduct oneself.

Initiating

To start the group working on the task based on the group's goals. However, if a problem or issue develops, use the group to find alternatives and strategies and still maintain the task objectives.

Respectable

To earn the admiration of the group as being a person whom they can trust.

Perceptive

To have the capability to recognize undertones in the group; using the positive ones to the group's advantage and ignoring or sometimes even countering the negative ones to diminish them.

Task Versus Process

To have the ability to know when to move through curricula and when to remain where you are in order to deepen the group experience.

Helpful Hints to Enhance
Your *Seeing Red* Group Experience

Recruiting Group Members: Be thoughtful about who you invite to a *Seeing Red* group. There should be a mixture of personalities and behavior variations in the group. For example, inviting only those who have a history of negative and chronic behavior problems would be a very challenging group to facilitate. Instead, include a member to serve as a role model, a member who tends to stuff their anger and needs to learn to better express their feelings and/or someone who would benefit from being in a group setting to enhance their self-esteem and leadership skills.

Emphasize the Positive: There is a strong thread throughout the curriculum stressing character building and positive leadership. Identify and point out the progress they are making and their healthy choices. This can really motivate the group to keep working on making positive choices.

Be Flexible: Even though *Seeing Red* provides you with a comprehensive plan for each session, allow your group members the opportunity to take the group where it needs to go. For example, if participants are really involved in a discussion related to the topic at hand, or focused on a particular activity, keep going and adjust the curriculum accordingly. Likewise, if an activity isn't effective or not working, move to a new activity.

Facilitator's Participation: Participating in the activities as a leader can be a great way to build rapport and trust. For example, if the facilitator draws a picture of what their anger feels like inside, just as they asked the group members to do, the kids likely will feel entrusted. Also, it can be a great way to role model the activity and what you expect your group members to do.

Be Prepared: Take careful time each week to read the session and gather supplies. As you get to know your group members better, you'll likely have a better of idea of what you think will work well and what might not. Keep in mind that curriculum is fluid and should be tweaked where needed to better fit the needs of your particular group.

Give Choices: Allow group members to make choices, too. Group members will invest in the group more quickly, as well as build their group decision-making skills.

Groups Are Unpredictable: One of the exciting aspects of group work is that every group has its own "personality." Some groups can be very challenging, and some seem to gel very quickly. Much of this is out of the facilitator's control and is related to the composition of a group. If your group is difficult or challenging, don't take it personally. Also, the "life" of a group can vary widely from week one to the final session. (See the "Group Process" section to learn more about group facilitation and working with kids in groups.)

Be Consistent: Be consistent with your meeting space, with who you invite to participate in the group, and how the group is facilitated.

Have Fun!

PART 2

Sessions

All the worksheets in this book are available for download at

http://tinyurl.com/SeeingRedWorksheets

Welcome to *Seeing Red*!

Lesson Objectives

→ Get to know one another and begin to establish trust.

→ Create group guidelines together.

→ Identify positive and negative reactions to the feeling of anger.

→ Introduce to group members that they will be building their "internal tool box" with healthy strategies throughout the weeks together.

Supplies Needed

❑ Blank paper for each group member, folded in thirds

❑ Markers, pencils/pens

❑ Group Guidelines sheet

❑ Set of Trash It and Recycle It cards for each participant

❑ Balloon and something to pop the balloon

❑ Dice

❑ **Tool Box Item:** Box to hold their tool box item each week

Preparation

• Read through the session thoroughly prior to the start of your session and be prepared to explain the tool box and its purpose throughout the sessions.

- There are many tool box options you can use to give to your group members. There are often inexpensive options at a dollar store or craft store. You can use shoeboxes and cover them with white paper.

- Copy the Group Guidelines.

- Copy and cut the Trash and Recycle cards so everyone has a set.

- Secure a quiet, confidential, and emotionally safe space for the group to meet each week.

Notes About the Session

The primary purpose of this lesson is to build group cohesion and lay the groundwork for future meetings.

Often times, participants assume they're in a group like this because of their frequent outbursts or bullying behavior. Regardless of whether or not that's true, it's up to the group leaders to reassure group members that the purpose isn't to focus on negative behavior, but to find healthy and helpful ways of helping one another make healthy choices when angry. Everyone can use this help. (Even us adults!)

Meeting Warm-up

10 min

A Name-tent Introductions

Welcome everyone to the *Seeing Red* group!

Give each person a blank piece of paper that has been folded length-wise in thirds, to form a "name-tent." Using the markers, ask group members to write and decorate their first names on the front of their tents. Also on their name-tents, they should draw two pictures of something about themselves to share with the group. (Examples: favorite food, a family pet, fun hobby they do, etc.)

When everyone is finished, ask each person to introduce themselves and share what they drew about themselves on their name-tent. Stand the name-tents up on the table so everyone can see.

Collect the name-tents after the session to use for the following sessions.

B Why Are We Here?

Many of the group members might feel upset or stigmatized because they have been referred to an "anger group", despite any attempts to frame it differently. It's important to address this as a way of building a fun and trusting space.

Emphasize the following:

- Reassure them that if they weren't able to control themselves they wouldn't be able to handle a group setting like this, and therefore wouldn't have been invited.

- It is a privilege to be asked to be in a special small group. Let them know it will be a lot of fun with many activities and games.

- This group can also help group members express their anger and not to stuff it. It could help EVERYONE, actually! (Let them know that you hope to learn new ways to help *you* with your emotions as well!)

C True or False Game

Group members take turns telling the group two things about themselves, one that is true and one that is false. The rest of the group tries to guess what is false, and then the group member reveals the answer before the next person's turn.

D Group Guidelines

Using the "Group Guidelines" handout, have the group brainstorm ideas for how they want to treat one another in group.

> *"If you were to look forward to coming here every week, how would we need to treat one another for that to happen?"*

Write their suggestions on the paper and ask all group members to sign the paper as their commitment to these guidelines. Be sure that the guidelines are present each week during meetings to serve as a reminder, if needed.

Be sure the following guidelines are included:

- **No put-downs or name-calling**

- **Take turns talking:** You may want to introduce a Talking Stick or ball with the rule that only the person holding the stick or ball can talk.

- **Confidentiality: "What is said in group, stays in group."** Give examples. Be sure to add that the adults must break this confidentiality if they feel that a child is being hurt, physically or sexually, or if there is a concern that a child is going to hurt him/herself.

- **Don't use names:** Throughout the sessions, participants will likely share real-life scenarios that have come up. Emphasize they should not use anyone's names who are not in the room, in order to maintain respect and avoid starting rumors/gossip.

- **Appropriate laughter:** You're going to have a good time, and there will be lots of laughter. However, laughing when something isn't funny can be like a put-down and make a person feel like they can't share.

Learning Activities

5 min

A **Trash It or Recycle It?**

Say to the group:

> *"Anger is an emotion just like any other. We all feel it—maybe even waves of it many times a day. It's not the emotion of anger that can sometimes gets us into trouble, but it's how we react to the emotion that can lead us to make bad choices.*
>
> *In fact, you can get in trouble for feeling happy! For example, if your teacher was in the middle of teaching a math lesson and you just remembered that your birthday was in 2 days so you shouted out, "Yay!!! It's almost my birthday!" and disrupted the class, you'd get in trouble, right? Well, the same is true when we are mad."*

Give a Trash It and Recycle It card to each group member. Explain that you are going to read many different reactions they can have to their anger. If they think it's a healthy or good reaction, they should hold up their Recycle It card. Conversely, if the reaction is not a good choice and can get them in trouble, they should put up their Trash It! card.

Option: If you happen to have recycle and trash bins in your room, you can have them move to either bin after you read the statements instead of using the cards.

After the activity, say to the group:

> *"Most of you had all the right answers! That was pretty easy, right? We know what we **should** do most of the time. It's just hard to make good choices when you're in the middle of feeling so mad!"*

Tell the participants that this *Seeing Red* group will help us practice with one another what they already know are good and poor choices when they are angry.

15 min

B Don't Let Your Anger Pop!

Hold up a deflated balloon. Now blow the balloon up just a little and use the balloon as an analogy for how to gauge big feelings.

> *"It's important to let our feelings out a little at a time so they don't get too big and makes us feel like we're going to pop— Like this..."*

Now blow the balloon up really big and make the connection of how if we allow our anger to get this big, it will pop or explode like we do in our anger sometimes.

Pop the balloon.

10 min

C Tool Box Introduction and Item

Throughout the weeks, group members will be building upon their tool box—both concretely and internally. Based on the weekly topic, they will receive an item that will serve as a reminder of the new skills they've practiced that week. They will bring this item home to place in their tool box they get today.

Depending upon the type of box you give everyone, give them some time to individualize their tool box by drawing pictures on it, words and their name.

Closing Activity

5 min

Roll the Dice

Ask group members to take turns rolling the dice. According to whichever number they roll, the person answers the question:

1. Who is a helpful person to go to when you're mad?

2. How can you tell when a close friend is mad at you?

3. What is something helpful you can do when you're mad?

4. How can anger be a helpful or useful feeling?

5. What did you like best about our group time today?

6. How do you know when your parent is angry?

Seeing Red Group Guidelines

Trash It or Recycle It?

Copy this page and cut out the cards. Every group member needs a set of both cards.

Trash It or Recycle It?

1. Teasing the person back. (Trash it!)

2. Ignoring them. (Recycle it!)

3. Putting my head on my desk and thinking about something peaceful. (Recycle it!)

4. Taking a deep breath. (Recycle it!)

5. Going to my room. (Recycle it!)

6. Slamming the door as I go into my room. (Trash it!)

7. Move away from whatever or whoever angered you. (Recycle it!)

8. Whispering something mean back to the person. (Trash it!)

9. Brush it off and later go to an online chatroom and tell your friends what happened. (Trash it!)

10. Ignoring them. Then turning to someone else and saying something mean. (Trash it!)

11. Telling an adult what's going on. (Recycle it!)

12. Running out of the classroom. (Trash it!)

13. Asking your teacher if you can take a break. (Recycle it!)

14. Grabbing the ball out of someone else's hands. (Trash it!)

15. Stuffing it for the moment and releasing it later by talking about it or doing something physical. (Recycle it!)

16. Stuffing it forever. (Trash it!)

17. Write or draw about my feelings or what made me mad. (Recycle it!)

18. Draw a picture of what my anger feels like. (Recycle it!)

19. Draw a mean picture of the person you're mad at and give it to them. (Trash it!)

20. Say something back to the person but without anger or attitude. (Recycle it!)

Session 2

What Are My Anger Triggers?

Lesson Objectives

→ Continue to build cohesion within the group.

→ Recognize how our anger is triggered in different ways and to varying degrees.

→ Identify the physical sensations of anger.

Supplies Needed

❏ "I Get Angry When…" list

❏ Yes and No cards (1 set per person)

❏ Copies of Me and My Anger Puzzle (1 per person)

❏ Markers

❏ Scissors to cut up their puzzles

❏ Envelopes for the puzzles (1/person)

❏ **Tool Box Item:** Me and My Anger Puzzle (1 per person)

Preparation

• Make enough Yes and No cards so each group member has a set.

• Make copies of the puzzle for each person, ideally on cardstock weight paper so it's easy to put the puzzle back together if they'd like. There are also packs of blank cardboard puzzles available to purchase at most craft stores.

Notes About the Session

Much like the last session, it is important to reiterate to the group that the feeling of anger is normal and okay to feel—even every day.

This session will focus on identifying what often triggers our anger. They likely will find that they have some similar triggers in common with others, which will help normalize their feelings and experiences.

In addition, group members will get in touch with how their body feels when they are angry.

Note: If you have a group with participants who are having difficulty focusing or following the group guidelines, you may want to give out stickers, stars, or some other small incentives to participants to reinforce their positive behavior/attitude.

Meeting Warm-up

10 min

A Memory Test

Before passing out the name-tents from last week, challenge the group to remember everyone's names and what they shared about themselves from their name-tents last week. Then hand out the name-tents.

If there are any new group members, be sure that they are given an opportunity to create a name-tent and introduce themselves.

B Group Guidelines Review

Review the group guidelines they developed during the last session. This is also important to do if you have any new group members. Have the guidelines visible and accessible throughout the session.

Learning Activities

15 min

A I Get Angry When...

Distribute a Yes and No card to each participant. Tell them that you are slowly going to read the statements from the "I get angry when..." list. After each statement, they should hold up either a Yes card or a No card, according to whether that situation typically triggers their angry or not. If the statement does not pertain to them, they should not put up either card.

Let them know that none of the statements you will read are funny, so it's important not to giggle or comment, as this could be interpreted as a put-down. Also, this is a quiet activity, and the only one talking is the leader reading the statements. Stress the value of everyone having their own feelings, experiences, and opinions.

Read the statements on page 32.

Follow-up Discussion

- What do you think was the purpose of this activity? (To recognize that anger is triggered by many different things.)
- Can you think of other situations that trigger your anger that were not read?
- What do you think causes us to get angry at some things and not angry at other things?
- Is it okay for us to feel angry? Why or why not?
- Is it okay to handle our anger any way that we feel? Why or why not?
- Do all situations make you feel the same amount of anger? Ask for some examples.

Say to the group:

> *"If you found yourself with your Yes card up for most of the statements, you may be one of those people who feels mad a lot. And anger takes a lot of energy and doesn't feel very good inside. So a goal for you may be to work on reining in our anger and channeling it only in places where it really matters, instead of every little thing."*

B Me and My Anger Puzzle

20 min

Ask them to shut their eyes, quietly take some breaths, and visualize their anger. Ask them to consider these questions in their head.

1. Where in your body do you feel your anger?
2. What color is it?

3. What does it sounds like?

4. What shape is it?

Now ask them to open their eyes. Hand a blank puzzle to each person and ask them to draw what they *feel* like when they're angry. Emphasize that the picture does not need to look like them, but should reflect how they feel inside when they're really mad. Examples: a volcano because they feel like they're going to explode, or a mousetrap because they feel like they just *snap* when they get mad.

Encourage them to make their pictures large enough to fill most of the puzzle so it's more fun to put together.

After they finish their puzzle, have them share them with the group. Then cut their puzzles up and put them into their envelopes.

Ask the group:

> *"When we feel our anger brewing inside of us, how can we stop it from looking like a broken puzzle or like the picture you each drew?"*

Say to the group:

> *"Sometimes our reactions to anger are so strong and forceful that we can feel puzzled or confused by them, much like a puzzle with its scattered pieces all over that makes no sense. Calmly, just like our feelings, we have put the pieces back together again so we can feel calm and clear-headed again."*

You may also want to add that putting a puzzle together can be a calming activity to do and something they might want to consider doing with their own puzzle when they are starting to feel their triggers.

These puzzles are their toolbox item to bring home and put in the tool boxes they received at the first session. The puzzle should serve as a reminder to keep clear-headed when we get mad.

10 min

C Keep It Below the Knuckles!

Say to the group:

> *"You're puzzle pictures are really great. And what you expressed in your picture are normal feelings when we are really mad. But*

*that kind of anger takes so much negative energy and can be
exhausting! Worst of all, it often leads to making poor choices.*

*So, we want to keep our anger in check, and not explode every
time we feel mad about something, especially when it's a pretty
small thing."*

Remind them of the closing activity during the last session when you
blew up the balloon really big and then popped it.

Ask everyone to create a peace sign with
their two fingers. Now, with the index finger
from their other hand, ask them to place it
across the knuckles of their peace sign.

Say to the group:

*"Now we are going to gauge our anger using this index finger.
Our goals is to 'keep it below the knuckles' as much as possible.
Of course there are unique times when our anger will go above
the knuckles, but those should be rare situation. Use this like a
temperature gauge, and you don't want to overheat. In our case,
we don't want to go above the knuckles, especially when you're
just beginning to feel the anger coming on."*

Closing Activity

5 min

Knuckle Check-in

Take turns having participants gauge their anger so far today using the
"keep it below the knuckles" tool they just learned. Remind them that
there are no right or wrong answers and that it's okay and normal if
they're "above the knuckles" today.

I Get Angry When...

1. I get teased about something I am wearing.
2. People talk meanly about my mom.
3. My family members argue or fight.
4. A pet dies.
5. No one seems to care about me.
6. My teacher yells at me.
7. I have to go to a new school.
8. I feel left out.
9. Someone tells me that I am ugly.
10. I have to do something that I don't want to do.
11. I get hit.
12. I feel like I don't get to make my own decisions.
13. I don't do something well.
14. My sister or brother teases me.
15. Someone close to me dies.
16. Someone I love drinks too much alcohol or uses drugs.
17. I feel embarrassed of my family.
18. I don't feel smart.
19. I don't feel listened to.
20. I'm not getting the attention that I need.
21. I don't see my dad.
22. I don't see my mom.
23. Someone causes me to cry.
24. I feel like I don't have any friends.
25. I get embarrassed.
26. There's nothing to do after school.
27. I have to go and live with a new family.
28. I work hard on something and no one notices.
29. When people talk about me behind my back.
30. When someone messes with me.

Yes/No Cards

Prior to the session, make enough copies for each participant to have a Yes and a No card. Cut them into cards for group members to hold up during the "I get angry when…" learning activity.

YES	**NO**
YES	**NO**
YES	**NO**
YES	**NO**
YES	**NO**

Me and My Anger Puzzle

Give everyone a blank puzzle. Ask each person to draw a picture of how they feel when they are angry. They will then cut the puzzles and place them in an envelope for them to take home. (See follow-up questions on page 29.)

Self-regulation: Brain Over Body

Lesson Objectives

→ Help group members understand that they can make good decisions, when they use their brain, not their body, even when they are really angry.

→ Practice self-regulation through calming breathing techniques.

→ Identify individual warning signs when they are feeling their anger triggered, in order to keep big feelings under control.

Supplies Needed

❑ Cookies or small treat, 2 per person (be sure to inquire about any food allergies first)

❑ Napkins

❑ Internal Angry Warning Sign cards

❑ This Is Where I Feel My Anger handout

❑ **Tool Box Item:** Small bottle of bubbles

Preparation

• Copy and cut a set of Internal Angry Warning Signs to make them into cards.

• Copy the This Is Where I Feel My Anger handout (1 per person).

Notes About the Session

Self-regulating their behavior may be very challenging for some kids, depending on factors such as their age, genetics, environment, and modeled behavior. But it can be done, and is what is expected as they get older.

For some kids, their anger can come on so fast and strong that they truly feel like they couldn't stop it, and therefore don't feel fully responsible for their behavior. The primary focus of this group session is to introduce the theme of self-regulation, reinforcing that they *can* and *need to* control their impulses.

As the sessions progress, group members will be building their internal tool box by learning and practicing more self-regulating skills.

Meeting Warm-up

10 min

A Who Wants a Cookie?

Ask the group if they would like a cookie (or some other yummy treat). Give them each a cookie, but before they eat it, make them an offer. If they want to eat their treat right now, go for it! But if they hold off, and not touch or eat their cookie for the entire session, at the end of the group they will get an additional cookie.

Some of the kids may choose to eat their cookie. If so, withhold any judgment about their choice.

For your check-in time, ask each of them to share either something fun they recently did, or something they are looking forward to.

B Group Guidelines Review

Be sure your group rules are available for everyone to see. This is a good time to emphasize one or two specific rules if there were any issues at previous sessions.

Learning Activities

5 min

A Stop Before You Cross the Street!

Have them place their cookie aside and introduce today's topic.

Ask the group to imagine this scenario:

- You're outside with your friends playing kickball at the park, and the ball rolls into the middle of the street.

- What have you been taught since you were very young about running into the street after a ball? (To always stop and look first.)

- Yes! But what does your *body* want to do as the ball is bouncing in the street, especially if it's a really fun game? (Run into the street to get the ball.)

- So your body really wants to just run out and get the ball, but what stops you from doing that? (Your brain stops your body because it knows the possible consequence of being hit by a car if you don't stop to look first.)

- Therefore, who has control—your brain or your body? (Your brain!)

- That is what you have to remember about your anger. You *are* in control of your body, even when you're feeling really angry and your body wants to explode. Just because your body feels the urge to throw a chair, insult a person back, or push your sister, doesn't mean it should happen. That's what your brain is for—to control your body.

10 min

B Baby Breaths of Anger

"Below the knuckles" follow-up:

- How did you do this week "keeping it below the knuckles?" (demonstrate the peace sign and index fingers again)

- Can anyone give an example of how they kept their anger below the knuckles when they got mad?

- Can everyone show me where they are today with their anger using their "below the knuckles" gauge?

Emphasize one way we can keep our anger below the knuckles is to focus on our breathing.

Say to the group:

> *"Everyone talks about 'taking a deep breath' when you're mad. Is that easy for you to do when you're mad?" (Let them respond.)*

> *"I think that can be really hard to do, but it also can be a helpful skill to practice and learn to do."*

Open a bottle of bubbles and blow some out. Do it again, but this time instruct them to look at your mouth as you do it. Give them each a turn, too. Explain that this type of slow, long breathing helps us calm our minds and bodies. Have everyone practice breathing this way.

Also, talk about how the bubbles can represent our feelings of healthy anger. When we feel emotions like anger, hurt, jealousy, worry, etc., it's important to express them when they are still small like the bubbles (or still "below the knuckles." Allow the feelings to come, recognize it, and then breathe it out.

Explain that they will get a bottle of bubbles today to put in their tool box as a reminder to take steady, calm breaths when their anger is getting big.

Option: As a way of getting out energy, have everyone stand up in an open area and blow bubbles to pop.

C Internal Angry Warning Signs

15 min

The key to preventing our anger from consuming us, or going "above the knuckles," is to recognize it before it gets too big.

> *"What are your warning signs that you are about to lose control?"*

Using the set of Internal Angry Warning Sign cards, place the cards face up around your gathering table. Ask group members, one at a time, to choose two or three cards that best name the internal warning signs they experience when they feel like they could lose control.

After a group member has finished identifying their warning signs and sharing about them, they should return the cards to the table so the next person can have the option to use them.

Ask the group:

> *"How can knowing your warning signs be helpful? (When you start to feel warning signs, you can do some deep breathing or use another tool to stop it before it get too big.)"*

D This Is Where I Feel My Anger

15 min

Give each person a copy of This Is Where I Feel My Anger handout. Based on the previous activity and discussion, ask them to draw a picture of where they commonly feel their anger when their warning signs are starting.

Ask them, "Where do they feel it and what does it look like?"

Note: You may want to have the Internal Angry Warning Sign Cards available for them to refer to as they draw.

Allow time for them to share their pictures.

Closing Activity

5 min

Cookie Time!

Acknowledge those who chose to wait to eat their cookie. Without shaming those who may have eaten theirs at the start of group, generally tell them that their waiting is an example of self-regulation. In other words, they were able to control their impulse to eat it, which in turn, is another example of the mind controlling their body.

Give them their bubbles for their tool boxes.

Internal Angry Warning Sign Cards

Feel hot	Surge of energy
Can't think clearly	Want to scream
Want to be alone	Feel like hurting the person
Feel like crying	Want to make the other person feel bad
Stomach turns or knots up	Head pounds
Can't get my mind off of it	Want to throw things
Body shakes	Want to run away
Feel "brain locked"	Fast breathing
Want to swear	Other reaction? (Not on cards)

This Is Where I Feel My Anger

Masking Our Feelings

Lesson Objectives

- ❏ Identify difficult feelings.
- ❏ Demonstrate how we cover up more painful or difficult feelings with our anger.
- ❏ Individually identify what "core feelings" we most often mask with our anger.

Supplies Needed

- ❏ Five paper bags (size of the bag may be dependent on the age of the group members)
- ❏ Wads of newspaper/recycled paper
- ❏ One set of Core Feeling Cards
- ❏ Paper plate and markers for each person
- ❏ X-ray Vision handout
- ❏ **Tool Box Item:** Paper plate masks

Preparation

- • On each paper bag write one of the following feelings: Hurt, Jealous, Happy, Calm, and Worried.
- • Using newspaper or recycled paper, make a pile of wadded paper balls for group members to toss during the warm-up activity.

- Make an angry face on a paper plate to show as an example and to use later when role-playing with the group.

- Make one set of Core Feeling Cards.

- If you plan to do the x-ray vision activity, make copies of the handout for each person.

Notes About the Session

This session helps participants recognize other feelings that are often masked or covered up by anger. Acknowledging these other feelings can help them to understand and normalize why they may feel angry so much. They can then recognize that they're actually feeling many other things, but transferring it into anger because it's "easier" to feel.

This session also encourages a deeper level of sharing. Be sure to remind the group about the importance of confidentiality.

Meeting Warm-up

5 min

A Feeling Toss

Using the paper bags, write one of these feelings on each bag: HURT, JEALOUS, HAPPY, CALM, and WORRIED. Spread the bags out on the floor or table. Ask group members to stand in a line several feet away from the bags (depending on their age/ability) and using the wads of paper, have them take turns shooting "baskets." After an attempt to make a basket, they have to tell the group the last time they felt the emotion that's written on the bag. If they make a basket, they have to answer the same question, but then have to ask another group member anything they want about feelings.

Note: Be sure to make this successful for all the group members so that everyone ends up making at least one basket. Also, role model cheering encouraging one another, and avoid creating a competitive environment.

Learning Activities

10 min

A Would You Rather

Read the Would You Rather statements on page 47. Group members who would rather do the first of the two choices should hold up a thumb.

Those who would rather do the second thing should put their thumb down. They must decide one or the other. Encourage them to think for themselves and not just do what everyone else is doing.

Option: Instead of using their thumb, they can also walk from one end of the room to the other in order to have them moving.

Continuing with the activity, adding these "Would you rather" questions:

- Would you rather feel angry OR would you rather feel sad?

- Would you rather feel angry OR would you rather feel lonely?

- Would you rather feel angry OR would you rather feel jealous?

- Would you rather feel angry OR would you rather feel hurt?

Say to the group:

> *"Feeling sad, jealous, or hurt are difficult feelings to have. Most of us would prefer to feel angry over these other feelings because anger feels less painful or raw. Because of that, we often mask, or cover up, these harder feelings with anger. For example, when someone calls you a name that hurts your feelings, you're actually feeling hurt, but we turn that hurt into anger because it's easier to feel angry than it is to feel hurt."*

15 min

B *Masks*-ing Our Feelings

Hand out a paper plate and markers to each person. Ask them to each draw an angry face on their plate.

Using the paper plate with the angry face drawn on it, demonstrate how people mask their anger. Whisper to a group member to say something to you (just for pretend) that would likely hurt your feelings. After they say it to you out loud, put the paper plate in front of your face to demonstrate how you covered your core feeling of hurt with anger. Do this with several different group members, using core feelings such as sad, disappointed, jealous, etc.

Note: Be cautious of having group members say these things to one another for fear of the words actually hurting someone's feelings.

Tell them that their masks are their tool box item this week to remind them to identify what core feeling is really under their anger the next time they get mad.

15 min

C Guess the Feeling!

Place the Core Feeling Cards face down on the table so no one can read them. Instruct group members to take turns picking a Core Feeling Card. The person who picks the card acts out the feeling while the rest of the group tries to guess which feeling it is. They should be encouraged to use words and real-life examples from times when they've actually felt the emotions to help them be more convincing and make it easier to guess.

For example, a group member who chooses the feeling lonely could say to the group, "I don't have anyone to play with. I feel like I don't have any friends." And the group either shouts out or raises their hand trying to guess *lonely*.

D X-ray Vision!

Keep the cards spread out on the table and hand them the X-ray Vision handout. Ask them to fill in the box with feelings they most often cover up with their anger, using the Core Feelings Cards as a reference.

OR

You Pick 'Em!

If you have an older group, set the Core Feeling Cards face up on the table and instruct group members to take turns picking two or three core hurts they most often cover up with their anger. Ask them to give an example of an experience they've had with each core feeling they chose. (Example: "I picked jealous because I get jealous sometimes of other kids who live with both of their parents.") You may want to go first to model how this activity is done. They should return their cards immediately after they've shared so the next person can choose the same card if s/he wants.

Closing Activity

5 min

Have them line up and give them each high-fives as they leave the room, telling each group member something they did well today during group.

Would You Rather

1. Go biking or go swimming?

2. Be infested by mosquitoes or by ticks?

3. Watch a movie or play a video game?

4. Have a sleepover or go to a sleepover?

5. Eat soup that had a fly in it or eat a chocolate-covered ant?

6. Be sat on by an elephant or swallowed by a whale?

7. Eat pizza or eat fried chicken?

8. Be known for your looks or known for your brains?

9. See a bear in a tree or be chased by a skunk?

10. Take the bus or take the train?

11. Take a math test or a take a swim test?

12. Do a craft or play a game?

13. Be captured by aliens or captured by zombies?

14. Lose both of your index fingers or 6 of your toes?

15. Be a famous musician or be a famous athlete?

Core Feeling Cards

Sad	Hurt
Scared	Jealous
Worried	Confused
Disappointed	Bored
Overwhelmed	Unimportant (or ignored)
Embarrassed	Other (not on cards)

X-ray Vision

Image by Andrea Gair

Not All Consequences Have Bad Outcomes

Lesson Objectives

→ Explore positive and negative consequences of our choices.

→ Help group members self-regulate by thinking through *all* their choices before making impulse decisions.

→ Problem solve difficult and challenging situations.

→ Understand that past behavior can't be immediately erased, but with work and perseverance, they have the power to make healthy choices most of the time.

Supplies Needed

❑ Slips of paper and pencils

❑ Markers or pens

❑ Consequence Scenarios

❑ Paper plates

❑ Beads for bracelets

❑ String or rope for bracelets

❑ **Tool Box Item:** Consequence bracelet

Preparation

- Make a copy of the Consequence Scenarios so there is one scenario for each person. Cut the scenarios and tape them up randomly around the room.

- If possible, make an Anger Pie about yourself to show and use as a model.

- Gather supplies for making bracelets, using any type of string and beads you choose.

Notes About the Session

Almost every decision we make has some sort of consequence. The intent of this session is to help group members anticipate possible consequences from the choices they make, both good and poor ones. In other words, instead of impulsively reacting to something or someone, they will practice thinking through situations and anticipate the many possible outcomes that could come from their choice.

Another part of this session is to help them better understand that their past behaviors or "reputation" has an impact on their daily interactions with people. For example, some group members may really want to change their behavior for the better, but the people in their lives already have their minds made up as to "who they are and how they act." This session addresses past interactions with people, and explores ways to help change that reputation, if applicable.

Meeting Warm-up

10 min

A **Guess Who?**

Give everyone a slip of paper and a pencil. Ask them to secretly write something about themselves they don't think anybody in the group knows about them. Collect the slips and read them off one by one. Group members should individually try to guess whose fact belongs to whom. To make it trickier, you can hand out another piece of paper so everyone can privately guess whose slip goes with whom and then reveal the answers all together at the end.

Learning Activities

15 min

A What's a Consequence?

Ask the group: *"What's a consequence?"*

Allow them to respond. It's very possible someone will say something like, "It's when you do something bad and then get in trouble for it."

Tell them with every choice we make there are consequences or outcomes. We tend to focus on consequences being negative because we are often told, "You need to think about the consequences before you act!" *after* we get in trouble. But we forget about all of the *positive* consequences that come from on our choices too!

Say to the group:

> *"Did you ever realize that most of our choices are good ones? It's true! We tend to focus on the negative consequences, but we make good choices all of the time. In this next activity, we are going to practice thinking through situations and anticipating all the possible consequences of these choices."*

Give each person a pen or marker and ask everyone to stand up and find a scenario taped up somewhere around the room to stand under.

After everyone is standing by one, ask them to read their scenario to themselves first, then write down all the possible positive and negative consequence that could come from the scenario. Emphasize that in most cases there are not only positive or negative outcomes, but usually some of both. (For example, a positive consequence of turning off your alarm and going back to sleep is that you got a little more much-needed sleep.)

When everyone is finished, return to your gathering space with the scenarios and take turns sharing their ideas. Others can offer ideas as well.

5 min

B History Counts!

- Do you ever wake up and think to yourself, "I am going to be really good all day. I am going to make good choices and try not get yelled at once by my teacher." (Maybe some heads nod.)

- It's mid-morning and so far so good. Then your good friend, who you sometimes get in trouble with for messing around, tells you a funny joke. You smile, but not laugh—thinking hard about your day's goal to avoid getting into trouble.

- But your teacher turns around and sees you and warns you *both* that next time you'll have to stay in for recess. You tell her it wasn't you, but you know she doesn't believe you.

- You feel so mad, and you think, *"Why do I even try? I end up getting in trouble even when I'm trying really hard not to! What's the point?"*

Help the group members understand that the history of a relationship matters a lot. If you *have* had a history of talking or messing around in class, it's going to take some time to change that perception. But don't give up!

Brainstorm ideas of how to recreate that history:

- Let the person (teacher, parent, friend, etc.) know that you are really working on this and want them to help you succeed.

- Keep your goals realistic.

- Keep trying! Try to avoid the mindset, "I'll try to make good choices and then give up as soon as I make a mistake." We all make mistakes! (Like the teacher in the scenario!)

10 min

C My Anger Pie

First, collectively make a list of all the various parts/places that are a daily or weekly part of group members' lives. Note: Some of these places will be a part of everyone's lives, like school or where they live, but other place may not include everyone, such as a faith community.

Some examples could include:

- Home

- School

- After-school program

- Sports teams, clubs, or other out-of-school activities

- Church or faith community

Next, pass out a paper plate and markers to everyone and ask them to make a pie chart that reflects where the hardest places (the biggest pie piece) and the easiest places (the smaller pie pieces) are for them think through the many consequences and make good decisions.

Example:

Tell them that it's important they realize where the places are for them where it can be challenging to make good choices because now they can be mindful and make a plan as to how they can think through possible consequences and make good choices.

10 min

D Consequence Bracelet

Have the group make beaded bracelets. They can be as elaborate or as simple as you want. Encourage them to wear their bracelets as a reminder to think through consequences of tough decisions before just reacting and then getting consequences based on poor choices.

Option: You can associate the bead color with broader concepts of what they've been working on in the previous group sessions.

Example:

Red: Is to remind me of our *Seeing Red* group and the support I have to make positive choices.

Yellow: Is for acknowledging that I'm getting angry, but know I can "keep it below the knuckles."

Blue: Is to remind me to cool down and breathe slowly.

Orange: Is to remind me to think through the consequences before I make a choice.

Green: Is to remind me to take responsibility for my mistakes and say, I'm sorry, when I need to.

Black: Is to help me think of someone or something in my life that makes me feel good.

Option: Test them next week to see if they can remember what each color means!

Let them know that their consequence bracelet is their tool box item for the week and should serve as a reminder to them to think through the possible outcomes—positive and negative—when making choices.

Closing Activity

10 min

"If You…"

On the count of three, ask everyone to hold up a number between 1 and 10. Based on the number they chose, ask them the following "If you…" question.

1. If you could watch your favorite movie or play your favorite video game now, what would it be?

2. If you could talk to anyone in the world, who would it be?

3. If you could wish one thing to come true this year, what would it be?

4. If you could have one special power, what would it be?

5. If you could have any kind of animal as a pet, what would you have?

6. If you had to be allergic to something, what would it be?

7. If you could be doing anything you wanted right now, what would you be doing?

8. If you could make a holiday come twice a year, which holiday would you choose again?

9. If you could eat your favorite food now, what would it be?

10. If you could learn any skill, what would it be?

Consequence Scenarios

Scenario #1

You almost always finish your homework and assignments on time.

What are the positive consequences of this choice?

What are the negative consequences of this choice?

Scenario #2

Your grandma repeatedly asks you to help her in the kitchen. You're watching TV and ignore her.

What are the positive consequences of this choice?

What are the negative consequences of this choice?

Scenario #3

A good friend asks you to keep a secret about someone they like, and you keep it.

What are the positive consequences of this choice?

What are the negative consequences of this choice?

Scenario #4

You play your video game after dinner instead of study for your spelling test.

What are the positive consequences of this choice?

What are the negative consequences of this choice?

Scenario #5

Your friend is teasing a girl about her looks, and you tell them to knock it off.

What are the positive consequences of this choice?

What are the negative consequences of this choice?

Scenario #6

You push your brother. He goes and tells on you, and you deny ever doing it.

What are the positive consequences of this choice?

What are the negative consequences of this choice?

Scenario #7

Your alarm goes off. You turn it off and go back to sleep, making you late for school.

What are the positive consequences of this choice?

What are the negative consequences of this choice?

Scenario #8

You are playing cards and have the chance to cheat, but you don't.

What are the positive consequences of this choice?

What are the negative consequences of this choice?

Bystanders

Lesson Objectives

→ Understand both the destructive and helpful role the bystander plays when someone is being bullied.

→ Explore concrete and helpful strategies to standing up to bullies.

→ Demonstrate the link between standing up for others and building confidence and leadership skills.

Supplies Needed

❏ Sticky-notes

❏ Masking tape

❏ 3 Hula Hoops (or draw 3 rings to use as a visual)

❏ Cheerleader, Do-nothinger and Hero cards

❏ Access and availability to the song "Brave" by Sara Bareilles

❏ Copy of the song lyrics to "Brave" (1 per person)

❏ **Tool Box Item:** "Brave" lyrics

Preparation

• Write the "Get-to-know-you questions" on sticky-notes and hide them around the room before the group members arrive. (Question suggestions can be found in the Warm-up activity description on page 60.)

- Make a line on the floor with masking tape—long enough for all of the group members to stand behind it.

- Copy the Cheerleader, Do-nothinger, and Hero page. Cut it into three different cards.

- Have access to the song "Brave" for group members to listen to, and provide a copy of the lyrics for each participant.

Notes About the Session

It can be very difficult for a young person to take a stand and defend someone who is being bullied, especially if the victim is considered to be "different" in any way. This session will acknowledge the courage it takes to stick up for someone. It will also identify the variety of ways a bystander can behave, and challenge group members to be a hero when witnessing bullying.

There are many reasons why people witness bullying but do not intervene. Many bystanders don't want to get involved for fear of being the next target. Others might not feel like it's their business to get involved. And some may feel like they could make the situation worse for the victim if they say or do something.

The role of the bystander is complicated and certainly is one that needs to be acknowledged and addressed in a non-shameful approach. Bystanders can experience feelings of guilt because they did nothing. If a victim is a friend or classmate, some bystanders choose to disassociate themselves from the victim. Others may blame the victim, with a "they asked for it" thought process.

Meeting Warm-up

10 min

A Treasure Hunt

Prior to start of group, hide around the room as many sticky-notes as you have group members. Participants should try to find a sticky-note, and when they do, they should return to your gathering table. When everyone has one, take turns answering the get-to-know-you question written on the note.

Examples of questions to ask:

- What has been a high point and a low point of your week?

- What's your favorite activity to do inside? What's your favorite activity to do outside?

- If you could be any animal, what would you be and why?

- How do you typically spend time with your family?

- If you could change one thing about your school, what would you change?

- Tell us something unique about your family.

- What is something you wish you knew how to do?

Learning Activities

15 min

A Over the Line

Ask everyone to stand behind the line of masking tape that was taped to the floor prior to the start of group.

Say to the group:

"I'm going to read a few scenarios to you about kids who are being picked on or bullied. Pretend you are a bystander, watching this happen, and if you feel like you should step in and say or do something about it, step over the tape."

Over the Line Statements:

- There are some notes going back and forth between a couple of girls. They are giggling and pointing at another girl as though it appears the note could be about her. You don't know these girls very well. Does this cross the line for you?

- You're in the hallway between class and you overhear some kids call your friend Kevin "gay boy" and laugh. Does this cross the line for you?

- You're in the hallway between class and you overhear some kids call someone "gay boy" and laugh, but you don't know him. Does this cross the line for you?

- You were on an online chat room last night and read some really mean things about one of your classmates being a fat pig. You heard them talk about it again during lunch the next day. Does this cross the line for you?

- There is new kid in your class, and no one sits near him at lunch. Does this cross the line for you?

- For about a week, a kid about two grades older has been teasing a boy on the bus, telling him he is poor and pathetic. You're the same age as the kid being picked on. Does this cross the line for you?

- Mr. Jones, the gym teacher, jokingly teases a couple of girls for how they dribble a basketball. After several day of this, you see one of the girls tear up and ask to get a drink of water. Mr. Jones doesn't seem to notice that she's upset. Does this cross the line for you?

- Be careful not to make any group members feel badly if they didn't step over the tape in any of these scenarios, but stress that in all of these situations it would be appropriate to step over the line and stick up for those being picked on or ignored.

Follow-up Discussion:

- It's not easy to step in and say something when others are being picked on or bullied. Why do you think it can be so hard to do? (You might be next! It's intimidating. You don't know what to say. It's none of your business. You don't want to be the tattle-tale, etc.)

- Do you feel you have a responsibility to step in and say something when someone is being picked on? Why or why not?

- When do you feel like it's none of your business to stick up for someone? Does it make a difference if the person being picked on is your friend? Why or why not?

- What about when it involves an adult, like the gym teacher Mr. Jones, in the scenario I read? Does that make it harder? How so?

- What are possible consequences of stepping in? (Remember, from our previous session about consequences, that not all consequences have negative outcomes!)

- How do you think sticking up for someone demonstrates leadership qualities?

Note: Emphasize that "stepping in" doesn't mean you have to always confront the actual situation. It's always an option to find a helpful and trusting adult who can get involved on behalf of the victim.

10 min

B The Role of the Bystander

First, using the three Hula Hoops (or your drawing of the three equal rings), make the following image for the group.

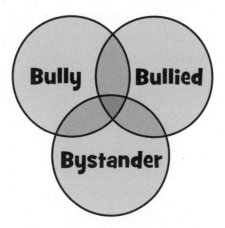

Help the group understand that, in a bullying situation, there are almost always three roles: The bully, the person being bullied (victim), and those that are watching or hearing it (bystanders). In most cases, bullies only bully if there is an audience of some sort because they like the attention and it maintains their social standing.

The bystander, or the witness of the bullying, has many choices:

1. They can do nothing and walk away.

2. They can laugh or add a comment or two, adding fuel to the bully.

3. They can go find an adult to help.

4. They can step in and confidently and respectfully tell the bully to stop.

Ask the participants if there are other choices a bystander can make.

10 min

C Cheerleader, Do-nothinger or Hero?

Briefly explain the three primary roles a bystander plays.

The Cheerleader

They don't actively bully the victim, but they are still a part of the action. They watch what is happening and are engaged in the situation. They may think what the bully is doing is funny, or they might laugh because they feel it is what is expected. They "cheer on" the bully by giggling or joining them with a "yeah!" which then encourages the bully to continue. They know that the bully wants an audience to display power and dominance.

The Do-nothinger

This person usually feels badly for the victim, and the bullying makes them very uncomfortable. They want to do something to help, but feel paralyzed to help. They may not have the confidence to stick up for them, or are fearful they will be the next targeted. They usually avoid the situation, just trying to stay out of it. They often feel guilty for not stepping in, and feel helpless to do anything about it.

(Be) The Hero!

Heroes will step in and confront the bully and respectfully tell her to stop, or they will immediately go and find an adult to help. The hero sees the injustice of the situation and isn't willing to ignore it. This person understands that the victim needs help, and they are willing to give it. This person usually has high levels of confidence and self-esteem. They get along well with others and aren't afraid that their friendships or social standing will be negatively affected if he stands up to the bully.

Put the three Cheerleader, Do-nothinger, and Hero note cards in the middle of the table.

To help them remember these bystander roles, read the various examples. The group should collectively point to the card that best fits the type of bystander: Cheerleader, Do-nothinger, or Hero.

1. He walks away for fear that he'll be the next victim. (Do-nothinger)

2. She stands tall, looks the bully in the eye, and with a calm voice, she tells him to stop. (Hero)

3. He snickers quietly at the insults the bully is hurling at her target. (Cheerleader)

4. He finds an adult who he knows will help. (Hero)

5. He walks away but later tells the victim that he's sorry that happened to him. (Do-nothinger—but an empathetic one!)

6. Her two best friends are in a fight, and she's stuck in the middle.

One of them threatens that if she talks to the other one she'll no longer be her friend either, so you agree, afraid of losing her friendship. (Cheerleader)

7. He watches a classmate make fun of their teacher for having a limp. He tells the classmate to knock it off, saying that she can't help having a limp. (Hero)

10 min

D "I Wanna See You Be Brave"

Listen to the song "Brave" by Sara Bareilles. Group members can follow along with the printed lyrics. (Not all of the chorus stanzas are included). As they are listening to the song, ask them to think about the role of the hero and the similarities to these words.

The lyrics should go home with them as their tool box item for the week, as a reminder to stand up against bullying and hurtful words.

Closing Activity

10 min

Compliment Game

Throw a small ball or Koosh to a group member in the circle and identify a positive characteristic in that group member, avoiding physical attributes and focusing on their personality or behavior. For example, "I think you are a good friend." Then that group member throws the ball to someone else and does the same.

After everyone has had a turn, close the group time by saying:

"It takes confidence to stand up to bullies. And we gain confidence by recognizing and acknowledging the positive strengths we have and letting others know what we appreciate about them."

"Brave"
by Sarah Bareilles

(The repeated chorus is not included in this copy)

You can be amazing
You can turn a phrase into a weapon or a drug
You can be the outcast
Or be the backlash of somebody's lack of love
Or you can start speaking up
Nothing's gonna hurt you the way that words do
And they settle 'neath your skin
Kept on the inside and no sunlight
Sometimes a shadow wins
But I wonder what would happen if you

Say what you wanna say
And let the words fall out
Honestly I wanna see you be brave
I wanna see you be brave

Everybody's been there, everybody's been stared down
By the enemy
Fallen for the fear and done some disappearing
Bow down to the mighty
Don't run, stop holding your tongue
Maybe there's a way out of the cage where you live
Maybe one of these days you can let the light in
Show me how big your brave is

Innocence, your history of silence
Won't do you any good
Did you think it would?
Let your words be anything but empty
Why don't you tell them the truth?

I wanna see you be brave

Reprinted with kind permission.

The Cheerleader

The Do-nothinger

The Hero

How to Keep Your Personal Power

Lesson Objectives

→ To discern how people provoke our anger as a means of control.

→ Problem-solve positive approaches to real-life situations.

→ Practice using calm words to diffuse potentially explosive situations.

Supplies Needed

❑ Pencils

❑ Toilet paper roll or paper towel roll covered in red paper to emulate a firecracker OR firecracker photo

❑ List of insults and comebacks

❑ Package of M&M's®

❑ My Personal Power Picture handout

❑ Markers

❑ **Tool Box Item:** My Personal Power drawings

Preparation

• Read this lesson plan carefully so you are able to really explain the important concept of keeping one's personal power when someone is purposefully provoked.

• Cover a toilet paper roll or paper towel roll with red paper and tape a piece of string to the end to look like a firecracker.

Option: If you aren't able to make the firecracker, you can copy the picture on page 76.

- Copy and cut the Insults and Comebacks into slips.

- Make copies of the My Personal Power Picture for each person.

Notes About the Session

Today's lesson is important in understanding the exchange of power or control that occurs when someone intentionally "tries to make you mad." The session demonstrates how sometimes people say or do things hoping to elicit an angry reaction from another person, and when that person reacts as expected, they essentially give up their personal power or control to them. In other words, the goal is to avoid giving them the satisfaction of reacting how they expect and want you to.

This concept may be a little complicated for younger participants, but the scenarios in the session should provide concrete examples that all ages can relate to and understand.

The group will also learn healthy and helpful techniques for handling such situations.

Meeting Warm-up

10 min

A M&M's Check-in Chart

Open the package of M&M's® and have the group members take turns pulling one out of the bag without looking at the color. Based on the color, ask the group member the following question.

Blue: Share a time this week when you kept your anger below the knuckles.

Red: Tell us about a good choice you have made today.

Brown: What is something you did or said this week that you wish you could take back?

Orange: How were you helpful to someone this week?

Green: When was the last time you told someone you were sorry? Tell us what happened.

Option: Let the group know that if they do a great job during the session you will give them some more candy pieces at the end of the session.

Learning Activities

10 min

B Diffusing the Firecracker

Put the firecracker you made, or the picture of the firecracker, in the middle of the table for everyone to see. Tell the group that in a few minutes they are going to role-play scenarios in pairs and the firecracker will be playing a role.

Say to the group:

"Ignoring someone when someone provokes you can be a helpful tool to use at times. But sometimes a person can be really persistent, and you actually need to use your words in order to try to stop them. Today we are going to practice doing that."

Before you begin the activity, introduce two tools that can really help prevent the explosive situations.

1. Use Humor: Make fun of yourself! (*Not* them!)

Example: "Tony, you're so dumb! You never get your math problems right!"

Possible Responses:

- "Yup! I'm dumb alright! I must've been born with an extra-small brain."
- "I know! I must've thought I was taking a spelling test instead!"

2. Turn It into a Question

Example: "No one wants to be your friend anymore because they think you're gay."

Possible Responses:

- "Why are you trying to hurt my feelings?"
- "I am wondering, how does a gay person act?"

B What's Personal Power?

Say to the group:

"Sometimes people hurt our feelings by accident. But other times someone says or does something hurtful on purpose in order to get a reaction from us. They just want to start something. Likewise, we sometimes do that to others."

Give the example of someone telling a classmate that they are ugly and no one wants to be their friend. They're likely not looking to make a friend. They are looking to get a reaction from them to make them mad.

Ask the group:

- If you give them the reaction they expect, who is in control of you? (**They are!**)

- And why would you want to give them your personal power, especially when they aren't being nice? (**You don't!**)

- But if you refuse to react the way they want or expect you to, you keep your personal power!!

Explain the importance of controlling their initial reaction of lashing back, even if they're steaming inside. It's like they have to be a really good actor sometimes.

C Role-play Insults and Comebacks

Pair the kids and give them a slip with an insult written on it. After they say the insult, make a sound like a lit fuse and say:

"The firecracker has been lit! Now it's your job to keep your personal power and put the fuse out. Remember the tools of humor or turning it into a question. Also, remember it's how you say it! You can't say your comeback with an attitude or the firecracker will explode!"

The rest of the group members watch the scenario and get to judge whether the firecracker diffuses or explodes. Other group members can also offer suggestions if the person gets stuck.

Note: Be careful how you pair kids. If two kids conflict at times, either in or outside of the group, don't pair them together or this could trigger a *real* scenario! Another option is for the adult to always be the provoker because the kids will likely not take the insult personally if coming from a trusting adult.

Follow-up Discussion

- Why does someone talk about someone else's mom or tell a person that they are poor or are a loser? (*To get someone mad.*)

- And if you give someone the reaction that they want, who is in control? (*They are!*)

- When you choose to ignore the person or pretend not to be angry, who is in control then? (*You are!*)

- Why do you think we sometimes provoke or purposely hurt someone else's feelings? (*Jealous, boredom, want the person to get in trouble by their volatile reaction, etc.*)

15 min

D My Personal Power Drawing

Give them each a copy of the My Personal Power handout and ask them to draw a picture of barbells or an image of power/strength. Then ask them to write inside the barbells or somewhere on their paper reminders as to how they can keep their personal power. Suggest that they place this picture up in a place where the reminders would be really helpful.

These drawings are their tool box items for the week.

Closing Activity

5 min

Who Helps?

Remind them that feeling angry is okay and it's important to talk about it and not to stuff their anger inside. However, you don't need to react immediately or react to the "provoker" directly.

Ask them to tell the group one person they trust and can turn to when they are in these difficult situations and can share their real feelings.

Insults and Comebacks

#1 Insult: "Your mama is like the sun—big, round, and hard to look at."

#1 Comeback: A. "That's funny. I didn't know you knew my mom."

                B. "Why do you care so much about my mom?" (Careful *how* you say this!)

. . . .

#2 Insult: "Why do you act so gay all the time?"

#2 Comeback: A. "I'm not sure what you mean by that, but it seems like you want to hurt my feelings."

                B. "I'm wondering, what does a gay person act like?"

. . . .

#3 Insult: "How could you not make that lay-up? My great, great grandma could've even made that basket."

#3 Comeback: A. "Sounds like we should recruit her!"

                B. "We all miss some once in a while."

                C. "Not my best shot, I know, but can't make them all."

. . . .

#4 Insult: "No, you're not playing on *this* soccer team. Go find something else to do."

#4 Comeback: A. "That's too bad because I'm feeling pretty good about my game these days."

                B. "Did I do something that makes you not want me on your team?"

                C. "Is there anyone else on this team I can ask instead?"

. . . .

#5 Insult: "Ha! You stink at spelling! Look at all you got wrong! That was the easiest test I ever took!"

#5 Comeback: A. "Small brain I guess."

                B. "Hey! Think you might want to tutor me?"

                C. "Thanks for caring about how I am doing in school!" (Careful of not having an attitude when you say this!)

. . . .

#6 insult: "You're so poor you can't afford to pay attention!"

#6 Comeback: A. (Laugh!) "Now I finally I know the reason why it's hard to concentrate sometimes."

B. "Wow. That's a good one!"

· ·

#7 Insult: "Don't even open your mouth. The sound of your voice hurts my ears."

#7 Comeback: A. "Sorry about that. I wouldn't want to cause any long-term damage to anyone."

B. "I'm sorry to hear that. Get it? *Hear* that?"

· ·

#8 Insult: "Oh man! You're in this group? I'd rather do this whole project by myself than be with *you*!"

#8 Comeback: A. "Can we just focus on what we have to get done?"

B. "Can you tell me why are you so mad at me?"

C. "Maybe you could ask the teacher to switch you to another group."

· ·

#9 Insult: "Monique just told me she didn't want you to sit near her at lunch because you were talking about her online last night."

#9 Comeback: A. "Thanks for letting me know. I will try to talk to her directly soon."

B. "I don't blame her if that were true. I hate rumors. I'll talk to her when I see her next."

· ·

#10 Insult: "You can't come to my house on Saturday if you stay friends with Paige. She was texting lies about me last night, and I'm not going to be her friend friends anymore."

#10 Comeback: A. "I really want to come over, but I'm not going to do that. This is between you and Paige."

B. "She didn't text me anything bad about you, and if she had, I would've told her to stop."

· ·

My Personal Power Picture

Session 8

Technology and Cyberbullying

Lesson Objectives

→ To discuss the use of technology in our world and name ways it can be helpful and harmful.

→ Learn tips for Internet safety and learn ways to be careful when using the Internet.

→ Define cyberbullying and examine the negative effects it can have.

→ Challenge group members to pledge not to participate in bullying of any kind.

Supplies Needed

❏ Two computer handouts: Some Great Things About Technology and Some Harmful Things About Technology

❏ Marker

❏ Cyber Pop Quiz

❏ Yes and No cards

❏ Access to the Internet to view a video clip

❏ Seeing Red Anti-bullying and Cyberbullying Pledge

❏ **Tool Box Item:** Their signed Anti-bullying and Cyberbullying Pledge

Preparation

- Copy the Some Great Things About Technology and Some Harmful Things About Technology handouts
- Copy and cut the Yes and No cards for each group member to have a set.
- The final learning activity in this session involves viewing a video clip from YouTube about saying no to cyberbullying. Preview this clip prior to be sure it's appropriate for your particular age group. Also, be sure you have the necessary technology available to watch it during your meeting.
- Link: http://www.youtube.com/watch?v=vmQ8nM7b6XQ
- Make copies of the *Seeing Red* Anti-bullying and Cyberbullying Pledge

Notes About the Session

This session is particularly geared toward older kids who access the Internet, online gaming, social media sites, text messaging, etc. There is a lot of information in this session, and depending on the age and engagement of your group, you may choose to break up this session into two. The topic certainly warrants attention, especially if you are working with older elementary or middle-school-aged participants.

There are a large number of active websites where educators, parents, and young people can learn more about the harmful effects of cyberbullying and how to stop it. Some of these websites are on our Resource List on page 133.

Cyberbullying is something to take very seriously, and plays a significant role in harmful bullying that can lead to devastating consequences, such as depression, anxiety, lowered self-esteem, and thoughts of suicide.

According to cyberbullying statistics from the i-SAFE foundation:

1. Over half of adolescents and teens have been bullied online, and about the same number have engaged in cyberbullying.
2. More than 1 in 3 young people have experienced cyber-threats online.

3. Over 25 percent of adolescents and teens have been bullied repeatedly through their cell phones or the Internet.

4. Well over half of young people do not tell their parents when cyberbullying occurs.

The Harford County Examiner reported similarly concerning cyberbullying statistics:

1. Around half of teens have been the victims of cyber bullying.

2. Only 1 in 10 teens tells a parent if they have been a cyber bully victim.

3. Fewer than 1 in 5 cyber bullying incidents are reported to law enforcement.

4. 1 in 10 adolescents or teens have had embarrassing or damaging pictures taken of themselves without their permission, often using cell phone cameras.

5. About 1 in 5 teens have posted or sent sexually suggestive or nude pictures of themselves to others.

Meeting Warm-up

10 min

A I've Never

Ask everyone to stand up from their chairs. Each person takes a turn saying something they have never done before. If anyone in the group *has* done what the person has never done, they should sit down. Before each person has a turn everyone should be standing up again.

Example: "I have never owned a pet." (Those who *have* owned a pet should sit down for a moment.) Then the next person takes a turn.

Learning Activities

10 min

A Introduce the Topic of Technology

"Today we are going to focus on how technology can be a great thing, and how it can also be harmful and hurtful if not used correctly."

Show the two handouts of the computer. Ask the group the question:

"First of all, how can technology like computers, the Internet, online gaming, and cell phones help us and be a good thing in our society?"

Write their answers inside the computer screen of the page that reads Some Great Things About Technology.

Examples could be:

- We have access to more information.

- Great tool for learning.

- It's entertaining.

- You can make a movie to send a message about an important issue (like an anti-bullying!).

- Video games are fun.

- You can stay better connected to your friends and family through texting and tweeting.

- Meet new people.

- Helps you find things like restaurants, stores, etc.

- A cell phone can help in case of an emergency.

Now ask them how technology can be harmful or hurtful. Write their responses inside the screen on the other computer handout that states Some Harmful Things About Technology.

Examples could be:

- There's less personal interaction with others.

- People can text or email mean things really easily and spread it to someone else.

- It can become addicting.

- You can be bullied online and not be able to stop it.

- You don't really *know* who you're chatting with all of the time.

- Some websites are not good ones.

- It can cause a lot of "drama" with friends and friendship.

Emphasize that technology can be and is a great thing in our world that helps us a lot, but we also have to be very careful of the negative things that can come from it.

10 min

B Cyber Pop Quiz!

Give each group member a Yes and a No card. Tell them they are going to have a pop quiz about Internet safety and cyberbullying. After you ask the question, they should put up their Yes or their No card.

Read the Cyber Pop Quiz starting on page 88.

10 min

C Defining Cyberbullying

Ask the group:

- What do you think "cyberbullying" means?

- What are the different ways a person can be cyber-bullied?

- Have any of you had personal experience being cyber bullied or doing it to someone else?

According to the resource, stopbullying.gov, cyberbullying is defined as bullying that takes place using electronic technology. Electronic technology includes devices and equipment such as cell phones, computers, and tablets as well as communication tools including social media sites, text messages, chat rooms, and websites.

Some examples include:

- Writing hurtful things through texting, online messaging, email, or online games.

- Posting hurtful and derogatory messages on social networking sites.

- Posting or sharing embarrassing or inappropriate photos or videos.

- Creating fake profiles in order to humiliate someone else.

Say to the group:

> *"The effects of cyberbullying can be really devastating and can effect someone for months or even years." Remind them of the consequence bracelets they made during the earlier session and how important it is that they think through all of the possible outcomes before they hit "send," "like," "open," or "comment."*

Group Discussion:

- What has been your experience with cyberbullying in any form? Has it ever happened to you? How did you feel?

- Have you ever cyberbullied someone else? How did you feel?

- Has a message that you sent ever been spread to others you didn't want to see?

- From 1–10, how big of a problem do you think cyberbullying is among your friends?

- From 1–10, how big of a problem do you think cyberbullying is in your school?

10 min

D Video Clip

With access to a computer, tablet, or smartphone, ask the group to watch a brief video on YouTube that some teens created about the effects of cyberbullying.

Here is the link to one called Cyber Bullying Virus:
http://www.youtube.com/watch?v=vmQ8nM7b6XQ

Note: You can also preview other options of anti-cyberbullying messages prior to the start of your group and show something else.

Ask them what they thought about the video clip they just previewed and how they can relate to it.

Have them brainstorm things they can do as a group to help with the issue of cyberbullying.

5 min

E Create Positive Change

Say to the group:

"The video clip we just watched is a great example of how technology can be used in positive ways. What can our Seeing Red group do to create positive change in our community and among your peers?"

Have them brainstorm things they can do as a group to help with the issue of cyberbullying.

Closing Activity

5 min

Anti-Cyberbullying Pledge

Show them the *Seeing Red* Anti-bullying and Cyberbullying Pledge. Ask them to read through it and challenge them to sign this pledge.

Be sure to praise them for being courageous leaders and peacemakers by committing to never bullying anyone in any form, or being a bystander in it either.

This pledge is their tool box item to remind them of their commitment not to harass, taunt, tease or humiliate anyone, whether in person or through electronic devices.

Some Great Things About Technology

Some Harmful Things About Technology

Cyber Pop Quiz

Q: You're online and you meet someone your age in a chat room. Should you give them your phone number and address so you can meet?

A: No! You're assuming they are your age, but you never can really know. You never want to give personal contact information to someone you've never met. If you want to meet someone offline, ask your parent or caregiver to get involved first.

Q: You're texting back and forth with a friend, and they text something really mean about a mutual friend of yours. You then forward that on to another friend so they can see what that friend said about them. Is that okay?

A: No! Sending hurtful messages, even if it wasn't you who wrote it, makes the situation worse and is a form of cyberbullying. You forwarding on the message can also be interpreted as you agreeing with the message, even if you don't. As a result, you then become a cyberbully yourself.

Q: You're texting back and forth with a friend, and they text something really mean about a mutual friend of yours. You immediately stop texting them. Is that a good choice?

A: Yes! You should never play a role in being hurtful to someone and don't want to condone the behavior by responding to the text. By stopping the conversation immediately, you are letting that person know you don't appreciate that type of text message.

Q: You meet someone in a chat room who lives nearby, and they want to meet. Should you agree, as long as you agree to meet in a public place.

A: No! You can't be sure of who they are, even if you've chatted online a lot. *Always* ask your parent or caregiver to be involved if you want to meet someone offline for the first time.

Q: Your best friend sent you a really embarrassing picture of himself because he knew you would find it funny. Is it okay to forward that photo on to your 2 friends who knows him well and know they would find it funny too?

A: No! You should never pass on humiliating, embarrassing, or inappropriate photos of yourself or others. After you hit send you can't ever control who will get the message. It can spread very quickly and be used to hurt or humiliate them.

Q: You're on the computer and you get an email to visit the fake website a classmate created with derogatory pictures and untrue stories about a teacher in your school that no one likes, including you. Should you hit delete and tell your parent right away?

A: Yes! Even by just visiting the website, you are sending the message to the author that you agree. You may not like this teacher, but no one deserves that.

Q: You get a text from a classmate that you don't really know very well who asks you if you are gay. Should you respond?

A: In most cases, No! Since you don't know this person well, you can't assume their intention by their question. This is usually a personal question and warrants a conversation, not something that is communicated via text with someone you don't know well.

8. Q: You've been playing a video game online with others all afternoon. You later check your email and see an unrecognizable email with an attachment to a foreign link. Should you immediately delete the file?

A: Yes! Corrupt or malicious programs may be hidden in game files you download or software you install.

Seeing Red
Anti-bullying and Cyberbullying Pledge

As a member of the *Seeing Red* group, I _____
pledge not to take part in any bullying or cyberbully.

By signing this pledge, I agree to:

1. Be a leader and take a stand against bullying and cyberbullying. That means not participating in or silently witnessing any harassment, taunts, or threats toward someone, whether in person or through technology.

2. Not to use technology as a means to hurt others, no matter how mad I might feel at someone.

3. Never take, send, or post pictures or videos that are embarrassing or humiliating of anyone.

4. I will think about all of the possible consequences before I hit click, and think through how my click might affect the other person.

5. Find a trusted adult to support me when I witness bullying or cyberbullying.

Signed by: _____

Date:_____

Session 9

The Power of Forgiveness

Lesson Objectives

→ Help group members recognize the importance of taking responsibility for their mistakes.

→ Demonstrate how asking for forgiveness and forgiving others is an important life skill.

→ Review the toxic combination of the bully and the bystander.

Supplies Needed

❏ Clear water bottle

❏ Food coloring

❏ Small syringe of bleach

❏ Paper hearts

❏ Book, *David Gets in Trouble* by David Shannon

❏ Markers

❏ **Tool Box Item:** Crinkled paper heart

Preparation

• In order to be affective, practice Learning Activity B prior to the start of the session so you know the proportion of food color to bleach.

• Copy the Paper Heart from page 96 so everyone has a heart.

• Purchase or check out from the library the book *David Gets in Trouble*.

Notes About the Session

Today's focus is on taking responsibility for our mistakes, and in turn, learning how to let go of grudges and forgiving others who have hurt you. It's important to normalize that we all make mistakes and we all need to seek forgiveness and forgive others at times.

The lesson is also a great opportunity to emphasize owning our mistakes in order to maintain trust with others. If we always blame someone else for our mistakes, for example, others might not trust us when we are accidentally accused of something we didn't do.

Meeting Warm-up

10 min

Sweet and Sour

Ask everyone to share something about their week that was sweet (positive) and something sour (negative).

Example, "The sweet of my week was earning my allowance, and the sour about my week was not being able to go to a birthday party I wanted to go to."

Learning Activities

5 min

A What's Forgiveness?

Ask the group what they think it means to forgive. Then ask them if they think it's harder to ask for forgiveness or to forgive someone else. Have them explain why that is.

Acknowledge and normalize that it is hard to admit our mistakes sometimes because we might be ashamed of our behavior or what we said or did to someone. Or maybe we don't want to get in trouble for something we did or said. Conversely, it can also be hard to forgive someone who has really hurt us.

10 min

B Cloudy or Clear

Hold up and show a clear water bottle filled two-thirds with water. One at a time, ask group members to share a time when someone was hurtful to them. Instruct them not to use specific names of people if the group may know them. After each person tells their story, carefully add a drop or two of food coloring to the bottle. Soon, the bottle should be very dark brown.

Note: Be sure not to add too much food coloring or the water will not become clear again.

Say to the group:

> *"So when people say or do hurtful things, it changes us. It changes how we feel about ourselves and others. Did you see how the water slowly got darker and darker? That's what happens when we hold in all of those hurts and grudges and we don't forgive."*

Now ask each group member to say a gesture of forgiveness to the person to their right, instructing them to speak with sincerity and looking the person in the eye. Acknowledge that this might feel awkward or silly, but it's important to practice forgiving others.

Some examples:

- "That's okay."
- "I forgive you."
- "I know you didn't mean it."
- "We all make mistakes sometimes."

After each person accepts an apology, add a little squirt of bleach to the water, using a safe squeeze bottle or syringe. The group will watch as the water becomes clear again.

Note: You will need more bleach than food coloring in order for the water to become clear.

Say to the group:

> *"When you forgive others or ask for forgiveness for the mistakes you have made, you can see clearly again and feel lighter and better. You no longer have this dark cloud of anger over you."*

5 min

C Chop It Up!

Ask everyone to stand up and spread apart from everyone. Now instruct them to stand with their legs apart and hold their hands high in the air, as though they were holding an axe. Now have them think of someone who said something that was hurtful or made them feel badly about themselves. On the count of three, say, "Now chop that away!" Group members say, "Yah!" as they throw down their pretend ax and chop the hurt away. Repeat this as many times as needed.

D Picture of Forgiveness

Give each person a piece of paper shaped in a heart. As you read the following story, ask group members to crinkle up a part of their heart for each hurtful thing that is said or done in the story.

> *Jacob was a ten-year-old, 4th grader who just moved from out of state, and today was his first day at Meadowbrook Elementary. When Ms. Thompson introduced Jacob to the class, Greg and Tony giggled quietly at Jacob. A couple of others joined in on the laughing, but a few kids smiled and waved a shy hello to Jacob. Jacob was so embarrassed he wanted to crawl under the desk and never come out. Ms. Thompson ushered Jacob to his seat and immediately started the math lesson.*
>
> *At recess Jacob stood against the wall and waited for someone to ask him to join in on the dodgeball game or toss the football with them, but no one did. The school staff supervising recess just let Jacob be by himself for the first day, especially since he wasn't causing any problems.*
>
> *In the afternoon when Jacob was in the bathroom, two kids guarded the sinks and wouldn't let Jacob use the sink to wash his hands. When they got back into the classroom, the kids announced to the class that Jacob didn't wash his hands after going to the bathroom. Ms. Thompson sushed the boys and continued with her lesson.*
>
> *When Jacob got home from school, he screamed at his mom, telling her he hated her for making them move and that it was the worst day of his life. On the way up to his room, he punched the wall and slammed the door so hard that a picture on the wall fell and broke.*

Ask the group to look at one another's crinkled papers. Ask the following questions:

• What were some hurtful things that happened in this story?

- We've named the hurts. But what were all of the opportunities in the story where there was a need for an apology or forgiveness?

- What role did the adults play in making this a harder day for Jacob?

- Do you think Jacob needs to apologize to his mom when he didn't have the choice to move or not? Why or why not?

- In the previous session, we talked a lot about the role of the bully, the victim, and the bystander. Can you name who played these roles in the story I read? How could this story have turned out better? What would each person have to have done differently?

Have the group un-crinkle their hearts, demonstrating that, after a sincere apology and act of forgiveness, you can feel like you have a full heart again, but you don't necessarily forget the hurts. That's why you can still see the crinkle lines on your hearts. It's another reason why it's important to think before we say or do something hurtful, but we all make mistakes sometimes.

Their crinkled hearts are their tool box item for the week, to serve as a reminder that we all make mistakes and we all need others to say "I forgive you" when we mess up.

10 min

D David Gets in Trouble

Read aloud to the group *David Gets in Trouble* by David Shannon. As you read the story, ask them to think about how much work it is and how stressful it feels to keep making excuses for our mistakes, rather than just saying, "I'm sorry," and starting over.

Closing Activity

10 min

Notes of Forgiveness

Get out markers and ask group members to draw or write messages of forgiveness on their hearts.

Heart Shape

My Family's Anger

Lesson Objectives

→ Help group members make connections on how their anger may reflect how their family members react when they're angry.

→ Normalize the many different ways family members express their anger, both positively and negatively.

Supplies Needed

- ❏ Playing cards with cards number 2 through 9
- ❏ Copy of Take a Step If
- ❏ My Family's Anger handout (1 per person)
- ❏ Pens or pencils
- ❏ Cereal box wrapped in plain paper (1 per person)
- ❏ Paper towel, wrapping paper or toilet paper roll (1 of each per person)
- ❏ Newspaper
- ❏ Packaging tape
- ❏ Markers
- ❏ Scissors
- ❏ **Tool Box Item:** Scream boxes

Preparation

- Copy the Take a Step If on page 102.

- You will have wanted to collect cereal boxes, newspaper and toilet paper rolls prior to this session.

- Also, you will have wanted to cover each cereal box with plain white or beige paper so they can decorate it later.

Note: The Scream Boxes are their Toolbox Item, although they clearly won't fit into their toolbox from the first session.

Notes About the Session

This session really focuses on their family's common reactions to anger. By exploring and processing how their household members express their anger (or not, in some cases), it can help normalize their own reactions, as well as recognize that perhaps some of the other group members have similar experiences at home.

Because this topic is a more personal one, you may gain more insight about what the kids are experiencing at home.

At the end of the session be sure to emphasize the importance of confidentiality, as they may have shared more personal things about their home lives.

Meeting Warm-up

10 min

A Deck of Sharing

Spread out eight playing cards (numbers 2 through 9) on your gathering table face down. One at a time, ask each group member to select a card and answer the following question depending upon the card number:

2. What has been the best part of your day 2-day?

3. Name 3 of your favorite foods.

4. On a typical night, what do you usually do be-4 bed?

5. Share a memory from when you were 5 years old.

6. How do you want to spend your 16th birthday?

7. If you were given $7.00 to spend today, how would you spend it?

8. Do you prefer to roller sk+8 or ice sk+8?

9. What were you doing at 9:05 this morning?

Learning Activities

10 min

A Take a Step If...

Ask everyone to stand up in a wide circle. Explain to the group that you are going to ask them to do the action you read, based on if the statement is true for them about their family's common reactions to anger. If it's true for them, they should do the action, otherwise they just stand in the circle. Read the Take a Step If statements on page 102.

After you're finished this activity, ask everyone to sit down at your gathering table. Explain that there were no right or wrong answers to any of the statements, but this is just a way to start thinking about how their family reactions can influence their own emotions with their anger, too.

15 min

B My Family's Anger

Hand out the My Family's Anger handout. Ask them to complete the boxes and allow group members to share their answers.

Note: Be careful not to make everyone share all of their answers, as some might feel vulnerable to answer, depending on their responses. You may want to suggest everyone share three of their boxes, and they can choose what to share.

After everyone has shared, help them see their commonalities as a way of normalizing their experiences at home.

Note: If they wrote down some personal and negative reactions at home, you may wish to collect their paper and not have them bring them home.

20 min

C Scream Boxes

Acknowledge that it can be really difficult to be at home where there is a lot of anger, negativity, fighting, or quiet tension. It can make it much harder for them to make good choices (although they can!!).

Note: Don't assume that there are difficulties at home, either. Just normalize this based on what they shared from their handout.

Explain to the group that they are going to make Scream Boxes to take home with them as one of their tool box items, so when they are really angry, frustrated, or scared, they can scream into their box and it will absorb their feeling and the sound that might otherwise get them in trouble.

Supplies: Covered cereal box, newspaper, paper towel or toilet paper tube, packaging tape, scissors, and markers.

1. They should stuff their cereal boxes with crumpled newspaper, but allow room for the tube to go through.

2. Next, cut a hole in the top for the tube. Close the cereal box and tape it shut.

3. Decorate their Scream Boxes however they want.

4. Scream into the box!!!

The Scream Boxes are their tool box item for the week, to use when they need to get out their energy or anger.

Closing Activity

5 min

Scream About It!

As group members should show their Scream Boxes to one another, allow them to try it out (if appropriate, given your meeting space), and ask them where they plan to store their Scream Boxes, as they obviously won't fit into their Tool Box they received during the first session.

My Family's Anger

I know my family members are angry when:

Something my family members do that makes me angry:

Some negative ways my family
members express their anger:

Some positive ways my family
members express their anger:

Some positive ways that I express my anger:

Take a Step If...

1. Take a step forward if the people you live with argue with one another almost everyday.

2. Touch your nose if the people you live with are really loud and emotional, but not necessarily angry.

3. Clap your hands if your family rarely expresses their anger outwardly.

4. Stick out your tongue if you sometimes don't feel safe at home because of the fighting.

5. Spin around if you sometimes don't want to go home because there is a lot of tension or arguing at home.

6. Touch your toes if you feel like where you live is peaceful and comfortable most of the time.

7. Cross your arms if most of the fighting at home is between your brothers or sisters (or other kids you may live with).

8. Hop on one foot if most of the fighting at home is between the adults you live with.

9. Squat down if most of the fighting at home is between the adults and kids.

10. Blink your eyes really fast if your family members typically retreat to another room and not talk to anyone when they are angry.

11. Tap your thighs if your various family members react very differently from one another when they're mad.

12. Make a goofy face if you feel like the way your family members handle their anger is a lot like how you handle yours.

13. Put your thumbs up if you feel like you handle your anger really differently than those you live with.

What Do *I* Ever Get to Decide?

Lesson Objectives

→ To help group members make the connection between their anger and the lack of choices they are allowed to make.

→ Brainstorm choices they *can* make despite circumstances they can't change.

→ Prepare for the closure of the *Seeing Red* group.

Supplies Needed

❑ *Seeing Red* Bingo card

❑ Pencils

❑ Set of What Choice Do I Have? cards

❑ Drawing paper

❑ Markers

❑ **Tool Box Item:** Journal

Preparation

• Copy enough Bingo cards for everyone to have one.

• Copy and cut the What Choice Do I Have? cards.

• Purchase a small notebook for group members to use as a journal to write their feelings out.

103

Notes About the Session

One of the things that can be very frustrating for young people is the lack of choices they typically get to make. Most of their day, they are told what to do, where to go, how to dress, what they can and can't eat, etc. Feeling angry about the lack of control or choices they get to make can be a real root cause of their anger. In this session, they will brainstorm ways they *can* feel some control and make decisions about situations they can't change.

It's also important to inform the group that next week will be the final Seeing Red session so they can be prepared. As a result, you may find some participants having a difficult time anticipating the end of the group, if they've come to trust and connect with their fellow group members.

Meeting Warm-up

10 min

A *Seeing Red* Bingo

Hand a Bingo card and pencil to each group member. Ask them to walk around the room and ask other group members something from a box printed on the card. For example, "Kim, do you like to sleep in on the weekend?" If Kim does like to sleep in, she should initial that box. If she doesn't, she can't initial that particular box, but can be asked something from another box.

The goal is for everyone to get a straight line of initialed boxes.

Only one person can initial each Bingo card, and you can't initial your own card.

Note: Be sure you have your group members ask others the questions from the box instead of simply handing them the paper, as this activity is about getting to know one another better.

Option: If your group struggles with reading, play the traditional version of Bingo where the leader reads the statement and kids can then initial the box if it's true for them.

Learning Activities

10 min

A Change Game

One at a time and taking turns, have a participant stand up in front of the group and slowly turn around to be inspected by the other group members. Then that person will leave the room and alter one thing about their appearance. For example, they could untie a shoelace, roll up a pant leg or take off a piece of jewelry. Then they come back into the room, and the other group members try to guess what they changed. After guessing, a new group member takes a turn.

10 min

B What I Can and Can Not Change

One at a time, read the following Can I Change questions and ask participants to clap if it's something they can change, stomp their feet if they don't have the ability to change that particular thing, and fold their arms if it's sometimes or depends.

Can I Change...

1. The weather (no)

2. My eye color (no)

3. My hair style (yes)

4. Whether someone I love has died or not (no)

5. Where I live (no)

6. Who I live with (no)

7. Who my friends are (yes)

8. What activities I'm involved in (some)

9. Whether or not I go to school (no)

10. What music I like to listen to (yes)

11. My skin color (no)

12. What I choose to eat (sometimes)

13. How I dress (sometimes)

14. How I choose to behave (yes)

Note: If you have an older group, instead ask them the question, "If you could change one thing in your life, what would it be?" You can also be more specific and ask them to identify a change they would make at home, at school, with their friends, or in their neighborhood.

Say to the group:

> *"We all know we have things that we can change, and choices we can make—like what to wear, music to listen to, how we choose to act with our friends, or even the mood we're in. But there are some situations we can't change, and therefore we can feel like we don't have any control. For good reason, that can make us mad!"*

Now ask the group:

> *"How many of you feel like adults are almost always telling you what to do, where to go, and how you need to act?"* (Raise hands)

> *"So today we are going to look at situations we can't change, and yet find small choices we can still make in order to feel we get to make some decisions, too."*

10 min

C   What Choice Do I Have?

Using the What Choice Do I Have? cards, help group members identify ways they can have a little control when they feel they have no choices in certain circumstances.

Place the cards on the table and ask a volunteer to read a card and ask everyone to brainstorm choices the person could make, given their circumstances. Then have another volunteer read a card, etc.

Here are some examples of suggested choices they could make from three of the scenarios.

Card Reads: Henry is really angry because his dad is in jail and he isn't allowed to see him.

Henry can't change the fact that his dad is in jail, but what choices can Henry make?

Some suggestions:

- He could write his dad a letter or draw him a picture to mail to the jail.

- He could have a picture of his dad, and he could talk to the picture as though he were talking to his dad.

- He could do something that he and his dad used to do together to help him feel more connected to him.

Card Reads: Jackie doesn't like her teacher and thinks her teacher yells at her more than anyone else in the class.

Jackie likely can't change classrooms, but what can she do?

Some suggestions:

- Let her teacher know she is really working on her behavior and hopes she will notice—this might help change the dynamic between them.

- She could write her teacher a nice note.

- Talk to her parent about it.

Card Reads: LeMonte is angry because he's moved three times this year and changing schools twice.

LeMonte can't be the one to decide whether or not he is moving, but what choices *can* LeMonte make?

Some suggestions:

- He can ask his parent or caregiver if he can visit his old neighborhood or school.

- He can get addresses or email addresses of the friends his misses so he can stay in touch.

- He can respectfully share how he feels about moving so much.

10 min

D Draw It Out!

Hand them each a blank piece of paper. Ask them to think and draw something in their lives they feel they don't have any control to change. At the bottom of the paper, ask them to brainstorm their own ideas of choices they *can* make despite a general situation they can't change.

Allow an opportunity for them to get advice or input from group members if they're having difficulty coming up with ideas.

Note: If they share something about their family that may be sensitive, give group members an opportunity to throw away (or you keep) their drawings.

E Let's Plan Our Party!

Because the next session is the last, take some time to get their input (where they get to make some decisions!) about what treats they may want to have for the final celebration.

Also, be sure to have the correct spelling of their names to put on their *Seeing Red* participation certificates for the final session.

Note: This can be a great opportunity to compliment the group on their decision-making skills and ability to compromise.

Move It!

Stand in a circle. Have each person come up with a physical movement and a noise and show it to the group. For example: spinning around and singing "Lalalalalalal!!," or doing a jumping jack and saying "Hey! Hey! Hey!" After the person makes their movement and noise, the next person does the first person's movement and action, and then creates their own. Keep adding on as you go around the circle so the last person has to do everyone's motion and sound.

Option: After one person goes, the rest of the group copies that person. Then after everyone has made their motion and sound, see if everyone can remember everyone's all together.

Their Tool Box item is a small notebook to be used as a journal. Let them know that writing or drawing can be a great tool to use for calming themselves, centering their thoughts, and working through difficult situations and feelings (including frustrations about the decisions they can't make!).

What Choice Do I Have?

Henry is really angry because his dad is in jail and he isn't allowed to see him.	Jackie is angry at her teacher because she thinks her teacher yells at her more than anyone else in the class.
LeMonte is angry because he's moved three times this year and changing schools twice.	Abdi is angry because as a cultural value Abdi's parents not to allow friends to come over to their house to play. Home is a place for only relatives.
Sam is angry because she has a new baby sister and she feels that all anyone cares about now is the new baby.	Marcus is angry because he is a slow reader, no matter how hard he tries. He gets pulled out to get special help each day which embarrasses him.
Tenisha is angry at her parents because she's not allowed to have her own cell phone and all of her friends have one.	Will is angry because his mom works two jobs and feels he barely gets to see her.

Bingo

Hand a Bingo card and pencil to each group member. Ask them to walk around the room and ask the other group members to initial a box from the card. For example, "Do you like to sleep in on the weekend?" If that person does, they should initial that box. If they don't, they can't initial that particular box, but can be asked something from another box.

The goal is to get a straight or diagonal line of initialed boxes.

Only one person can sign each Bingo card. You can't sign your own card.

BINGO

You have your own email address	You save more money than spend it	You play at least one sport	You like to draw or write in a journal	You forgot to brush your teeth today
You were born in a different state or country	You want to be famous someday	You like cookies more than chips	You have had stitches before	You live with a grandparent
Reading is one of your favorite parts of school	You have been to a summer camp before	FREE SPACE	You have 3 or more siblings	You've had pizza in the past week
You ate cereal this morning for breakfast	You speak another language at home	You don't know how to swim	Your favorite color is red	You play an instrument
You like to play video games	You have a pet	You like to sleep in on the weekend	You have been on an airplane	You share a bedroom with at least one other person

Seeing Red Good-bye Celebration!

Lesson Objectives

→ Acknowledge and celebrate the growth and improvement of each *Seeing Red* member.

→ Identify others in their lives who can help them remember and practice the many skills they have learned throughout the sessions.

→ Give group members the opportunity to evaluate their *Seeing Red* experience.

→ Remind participants of their tool box skills they have learned and/or identified.

→ Bring closure to the group and celebrate the group members' participation.

Supplies Needed

❏ *Seeing Red* tool box items

❏ Helping Hand handout

❏ Personalized Certificate of Participation

❏ Final Evaluation handout or cardstock paper

❏ Pencils

❏ Snack food for the party

❏ Music for the party (optional)

❏ **Tool Box Item:** List of Seeing Red Tool Box Items

Preparation

- Review the Seeing Red Tool Box Items correlating the session week with tool box item. Make a copy for each person to take home with them.

- Copy the Helping Hand for each group member.

- Copy the Final Evaluation for each person to complete OR have a piece of cardboard or cardstock available for each person.

- Prepare a Certificate of Participation for each group member prior to the meeting.

- Gather snack food for the final celebration.

Notes About This Session

The final session has many goals. First, the session will help group members recognize their progress throughout the previous group sessions. Second, participants will have an opportunity to evaluate their group experience. Thirdly, they can identify people in their lives who can help them continue to make healthy choices, and bring closure to the group and their individual experience. And last, participants will celebrate their group experience with a small party.

Meeting Warm-up

5 min

Tool Box Review

Collectively ask everyone if they can remember all of the tool box items from all the previous sessions. (Facilitators can have a "cheat sheet" by referring to the Seeing Red Tool Box Items handout.)

Learning Activities

10 min

A Tool Box Review

Give them the handout of the tool box items they have received over the sessions.

Note: If you haven't completed 12 sessions, highlight the tool box items you have focused on throughout your *Seeing Red* group.

Here is a list of the tool box items they have been building and working on throughout their *Seeing Red* experience:

Session 1: Tool box

Session 2: Me and My Anger Puzzle drawing

Session 3: Bubbles

Session 4: Paper plate masks

Session 5: Consequence Bracelets

Session 6: "Brave" lyrics

Session 7: My Personal Power drawing

Session 8: Anti-bullying and Cyberbullying Pledge

Session 9: Crinkled paper heart

Session 10: Scream Boxes

Session 11: Journal

Session 12: List of *Seeing Red* Tool Box Items

Ask them to identify the top three tools or skills they have practiced the most and identify two skills that they have used the least. Ask them why they think that is.

10 min

B Helping Hand

Give each participant a copy of the Helping Hand handout and ask them to decorate their hand and identify people who can continue to help them to make positive choices and practice the skills they have practiced and learned from their *Seeing Red* group. Challenge them to think of people in different parts of their lives like home, school, friends, after school activities, etc.

Give them an opportunity to tell the group who those people are for them.

15 min

C Final Evaluation

Give them the Final Evaluation handout and instruct them to individually complete the evaluation, being as truthful and thorough as possible. Once group members have finished their evaluation, ask them to choose any two questions from their evaluation they would like to share.

Note: If the group doesn't have well-developed reading/writing skills, the leaders should read the evaluation questions aloud and provide necessary assistance to group members.

OR

Give each of them a piece of cardstock paper and ask them to write a word or draw a picture of what they remember feeling on the first day of the *Seeing Red* group. Then, ask them to turn over the cardboard and write a word or draw a picture of how they feel about their *Seeing Red* group today. Ask them to share their words/drawings with the group.

5 min

D Group Closing

Present each participant with a certificate that states they have successfully completed the *Seeing Red* group.

15 min

Party Time!

Provide some treats and perhaps some fun music to celebrate the *Seeing Red* group and all they have accomplished.

As they are eating, ask each person to say one positive thing about their group experience.

As they walk out the door (with their Helping Hand handout and list of tool box items in hand), give them a high five and tell each of them one thing you have noticed they have improved or done a great job practicing regarding their behavior, choices, or self-regulation skills.

Seeing Red Final Evaluation

Today is the last day of group.

I feel _____ and _____ to see it end.

Two things we did in this group that I liked were:

1. _____

2. _____

I had many different feelings during the group. Some of the feelings I had were:

_____   _____

_____   _____

Some important things I learned about my anger were:

_____

_____

Something I still wonder about related to my anger is:

_____

_____

Some skills I learned in order to control my anger are:

_____

_____

I plan to continue to work on making good choices by:

_____

_____

Seeing Red Tool Box Items

Session 1: TOOL BOX
A box to store your tool box items

Session 2: ME AND MY ANGER PUZZLE
To remind you to keep clear-headed when you're feeling angry.

Session 3: BUBBLES
To remind you to take steady, calm breaths when your anger feels big.

Session 4: PAPER PLATE MASKS
To remind you to identify the core feelings you may be masking with anger.

Session 5: CONSEQUENCE BRACELETS
To remind you to think through all possible consequences, both positive and negative.

Session 6: LYRICS TO THE SONG "BRAVE"
To remind you to stand up against bullying and hurtful words.

Session 7: MY PERSONAL POWER DRAWING
To remind you of the different ways you can keep your personal power when being provoked by someone.

Session 8: ANTI-BULLYING/CYBERBULLYING PLEDGE
To remind you of your commitment not to harass, taunt, teases or humiliate anyone, either in person or through any technology.

Session 9: CRINKLED PAPER HEART
To remind you that we all make mistakes and the importance of saying "I'm sorry" and "I forgive you."

Session 10: SCREAM BOXES
To use when you need to let big feelings out.

Session 11: JOURNAL
To remind you that writing or drawing is a great outlet to express your feelings and experiences.

Session 12: LIST OF TOOL BOX ITEMS
To serve as a reminder of what all of your tool box items symbolize.

Helping Hand

Trace your hand and write inside it the names of people you can turn to for support and help you continue to make good choices.

CERTIFICATE OF PARTICIPATION

_____

is recognized for participating
in the SEEING RED group

_____

Leader's Name   **Date**

_____

Leader's Name   **Date**

Affirmations

I acknowledge that I am feeling angry right now, and accept the way I feel.

I have the power to control my actions.

I know I can feel a lot of anger, and I have the ability to wait before I react.

I know that my brain controls my body.

I can feel angry, but in control at the same time.

I know that it's okay to feel angry.

I can release my anger in healthy ways.

I choose to live my life the way that makes me happy and healthy.

When I don't make a good choice, I can forgive myself and try again.

I love and accept myself as I am.

I work hard to be respectful of others.

I am respectful of others, even if I don't agree with them.

I am a good friend to others, and I know I deserve good friends, too.

I forgive those that need my forgiveness, and I forgive myself.

The more grudges I let go of, the freer and happier I feel.

I can tell I am making better and better choices everyday.

I know I don't need to hurt someone's feelings just because my feelings are hurt.

I can stay calm during stressful or difficult situations.

I am a well-loved and well-respected person.

I am free to make my own choices and decisions.

I know I am responsible for my mistakes, and for what I do well.

I understand that there are positive consequences to my positive choices.

I have the courage to make positive choices in my life.

I am a thoughtful and caring person.

I can allow myself to feel angry and peacefully let it go.

I make the decision not to tease someone or hurt their feelings.

I stick up for others who are teased or bullied.

I can identify people in my life who help me make good choices and who care about me.

I have the ability to think before I act, making sure I don't hurt someone's feelings.

Supplemental *Seeing Red* Activities and Self-regulation Techniques

Knowing the skills, interests, and "personality" of your group, you may want to substitute or add particular activities or components to your sessions.

General Ideas to Incorporporate in Your *Seeing Red* Group

The following are suggestions of things you can routinely include in your *Seeing Red* group each session.

Affirmations

Begin or end each session with each group member reading an affirmation. They can add these affirmations to their tool box each week. A list of affirmations can be found on page 119.

Option: After the group gets the hang of these, challenge them to create affirmations for one another.

What's Your #1 Goal?

Early on, ask group members to identify one specific goal to work on in regards to their anger. Ask them to choose a goal that really would help them in making positive choices. One way to frame the question could be, "If I had a magic wand in my hand right now, and with one swish of the wand I could make something that's a struggle for you related to your anger or behavior just disappear, what would you choose to change? Perhaps something that commonly gets you in trouble?"

Have them identify this goal at the first or second session. Write down their goal and brainstorm ways to help them achieve this goal. They can work toward this goal throughout the many sessions. Parents and teachers could be involved in helping them work on their goal outside of the *Seeing Red* group.

Sentence Starters

Begin each group with a sentence starter that they complete.

Examples of some sentence starters:

- Something I really like about winter is…

- I'm looking forward to…

- If I could have any animal as a pet, I would have…

- My favorite restaurant is…

- On a rainy Saturday, I like to…

- Something I like to do with my family is…

- Something I like to do with my friends is…

Creat a Quiet Space

Before group members arrive, create a quiet and welcoming space that reflects the tone you hope they will bring into the group. As the weeks progress, you will likely see group members walk into the room more calmly and quietly as a result.

Some examples could include:

- Soft lighting: use lamps instead of overhead lights.

- Light a candle in the middle of your table. (You can purchase inexpensive candles that have a bulb instead of a flame).

- Play soothing music as they enter the space.

- Start every session with a simple yoga pose, affirmation, or one minute of mindful breathing to center the group.

Peace Stick

If your group struggles with participants commonly interrupting one another or only one or two participants doing all of the talking, create a *Seeing Red* peace stick. Only the person holding the stick can talk.

Option: Use the peace stick only in certain activities in the session to allow for more free flowing discussion.

Shake It Out!

Supplies: Small empty bottle, rice, duct tape, and a permanent marker

Fill a small bottle about halfway with rice (or dry beans, beads, etc.). Close the bottle and wrap the whole thing in (red!) duct tape. Write "SHAKE IT OUT!" on the outside. Start your group each week asking everyone to "Shake it out!" i.e., shaking out any anger they may be carrying with them that day.

Option: You can do this as a craft project where everyone makes one and can bring it home with them as a tool to use when they are mad.

Additional Warm-up/Team Building Activities

Who Am I?

Using masking tape or mailing labels, write the name of a famous person on each person's back, but don't let them see it. The person could be fictitious, someone who died long ago, a famous actor, singer, etc. (Just be sure it's someone everyone likely knows.) When everyone has a label on their back, they should mingle around the room and try to figure out who "they are" by asking their group members only yes or no questions. For example, "Am I alive?" or "Have I ever been in a movie?" To help them get to know one another better, they can only ask the same person three questions before moving on to someone else.

Seeing Red Band Concert

Ask everyone to choose an instrument to "play." Then act like the conductor, and when you point to a person, they start making the sound of their instrument. Then have another group member start "playing" their instrument. You can direct them to play louder, then softer, etc. Eventually everyone should be playing together (although it might not sound very good!). Allow them to take turns being the conductor and/or changing their instruments. Compliment them for following directions, being a follower, and being a leader—all important skills that *Seeing Red* members are working on.

Paper Cup Check-in

Using a large plastic cup, ask group members to check in by instructing them to place the cup upside down if they've had a rough day/week, or up if they've had a good day/week. They can also place it on its side if it has been an "in-between" week. Ask them to explain why.

Option: This can be something you can do just once, or do routinely. If you choose to make this a part of many sessions, it could be fun to decorate the cup together and have them sign their name on it to make it more personal.

Wind in My Sail

Ask group members to check in about their anger using the metaphor of wind. Are you having a windless day, a soft breeze day, a really windy day, or are you experiencing hurricane/tornado winds?

Option: Have them use their bodies and sounds to describe the kind of "windy day" they are having.

Additional Learning Activities Specific to Anger and Behaviors

Group Punching Bag

Supplies: Trash can, plastic trash bag, pile of newspapers, and duct tape

Line a small or medium-sized wastebasket with a plastic bag. Using lots of recycled newspaper, have the kids wad up the paper into balls and throw it into the trash as hard as they can. Everyone can do this all together until the trash is almost filled. Then pull the bag out and tie it with duct tape. Wrap the entire bag with duct tape and you have created a *Seeing Red* punching bag! Take turns punching the bag while saying something that makes them feel angry.

Mad Targets

Supplies: A bull's-eye target, tape, and ping-pong balls

Tape on a wall or ceiling a picture of a target with a bull's-eye. Have kids stand back and try to hit the target with ping-pong balls, or some other light object, depending on what you use for a target. After they hit their target, ask them to finish a statement about their anger.

Suggested Statements:

1. When I get mad I really feel it in my _____.

2. Something that helps me feel better when I'm mad is _____.

3. It's easiest for me to make good choice when I _____.

4. A safe person I can talk to about my feelings is _____.

5. The last time I felt proud of myself was _____.

6. I show I'm a good friend to others by _____.

7. I feel most calm when I'm _____.

8. I wish others would understand _____ about me.

9. A person I admire is _____ because _____.

Jenga® With A Twist

Supplies: wood block game

Using a wood block game such as Jenga®, players carefully pull out a wooden block from the stack and set it on top without causing the stack to fall. (Play the game by the printed rules.) However, after they successfully have placed their block on top of the stack, they have to finish the Wood Block Statement found on page 131 before the next person has a turn. Whoever makes the stack fall has to share three things about themselves that the group does not already know.

Tornado Shaker

Supplies: Tape, clear water bottle, baby oil, glitter, beads, small rocks

Using a clear water bottle, fill it with water and add some baby oil to help make items float. Then add the glitter, beads, rocks, etc. Securely tape the cap on the bottle.

Use this tornado shaker as a visual about how our anger can feel very out of control and chaotic (shake it up), then set the shaker on the table and carefully watch all the items slowly float to the bottom. Let them know that they are practicing patience and calmness as they watch the items settle, which is an important skill.

Mandalas

If your group needs a calming activity, or if you have participants who trickle in at different times, offer them a mandala to color. It can be very calming and even meditative. *Mandala* is a Sanskrit word that means "circle." They are abstract designs that are most often circular. Mandalas usually have one identifiable center point. There are many options of mandalas you can print and copy from the Internet. Be sure you print mandalas that are at age level for your group.

Colormandala.com is just one website suggestion.

Anti-bullying Public Service Announcement

As a project for their school or program, encourage group members to create a PSA about anti-bullying and anti-cyberbullying. They could make posters to put up, make a video, create a song, poem, etc.

Letter of Gratitude

Supplies: Paper, pens/markers

It can be helpful to focus on the positive things in our lives in order to pull ourselves out of the "victim mentality." Ask everyone to write a letter or draw a picture of gratitude to someone who has helped them, supported them, or just someone they are grateful to know. Encourage them to send the letter (or offer to mail it for them).

Option: Close the session each week with everyone writing 3–5 things they are thankful for in their lives. It can be as simple as, "I'm grateful for recess!"

Your Inner Animal

Supplies: Some modeling clay for each person

Give everyone some clay or Play-doh®. Ask them to sculpt an animal that best represents their anger. For example, a lion could symbolize how you yell or "roar" when you're mad. Or a bird could represent how someone wants to flee the situation when they get mad.

Letter Writing

Supplies: Paper and pens

If you have an older group, ask them to write a letter to someone they feel angry at quite often. Challenge them to write a respectful letter about their feelings and interactions with this person, and not write a letter that's mean-spirited or accusatory.

Suggest this sentence prompt:

"I feel _____ when you _____ because _____. And I want _____." Give them the option to keep the letter or give it to the person.

Toss It!

Supplies: Rocks and permanent markers

Give everyone two or three rocks. Using a permanent marker (a silver metallic marker is ideal), have group members write a regret they have or a grudge they're holding onto on the rocks. When everyone has at least one rock, go outside and find a space where they can safely throw their rocks as far as they can. Emphasize the importance of letting go of regrets or grudges because carrying those around—just like rocks, are heavy and can weigh us down.

Additional Self-regulation and Self-calming Techniques

If you would like to focus more attention on building their skills to self-regulate their behavior through calming techniques, the following are some additional activities to incorporate.

Belly Breathing

Supplies: Open floor space and a small stuffed animal for each person to use.

If your space allows, ask everyone to lie down on the ground on their backs. Then place a small stuffed animal on each of their bellies. Guide them to slowly breathe using their bellies. They should be able to breathe so the stuffed animal comes up and "greets them" with their eyes. That indicates they are using the correct calming and centering of breathing.

Yoga Mountain Pose

The mountain pose can be very helpful in grounding and centering the group, and something you can do each week as a ritual to begin or end your session. The pose is easy to learn, easy to practice and can be used in almost every environment.

Here is how it's done.

1. Spread feet slightly apart and even, with toes pointed straight ahead. (They can have their feet together as they practice more and feel more balanced.)

2. Spine straight

3. Stomach strong

4. Chin is up and level

5. Eyes are focused forward

6. Arms are resting at sides

7. Heels and toes are pressed down into the ground

Encourage them to use the mountain pose anytime when they feel fidgety or anxious

More Breathing Techniques

Other objects you can use to help group members self-regulate using their breath (in addition to using bubbles in Session 3):

1. Blowing a spinwheel with a steady breath to make it spin at varied speeds

2. Using a straw, blow a ping-pong ball across a table or rug

3. Hold a feather in front of their mouths and see how they can make the feather move just a little, or can even bend it when using a strong breath

Strong Voice, Calm Voice

Have participants shut their eyes and ask them to locate their strong voice inside. Ask them the following questions for them to answer in their head:

1. Where do you feel the strong voice in your body?

2. Is the voice high or low?

3. Is the voice loud or soft?

4. What does the voice remind you of?

5. What does the voice say?

6. What can you do to find your strong voice when you are angry or afraid?

7. When do you need your strong voice?

Have them open their eyes and draw a picture of themselves feeling strong.

Ask them to shut their eyes again, but this time locate their calm voice inside.

1. Where do you feel the calm voice in your body?

2. Is the voice high or low?

3. Does the voice talk fast or slow?

4. What does the calm voice sound like?

5. What does the calm voice say?

6. What are the places you go to help you hear your calm voice?

7. When can a calm voice help you?

8. Have them open their eyes and draw a picture of themselves feeling strong.

Another Viewpoint

Say to the group:

"Picture in your head a little 2- or 3-year-old. Maybe your cousin or your little brother or sister, or a family friend.

Now imagine this 2-year-old pushing a friend because she or he took their toy. That would be pretty normal for a toddler to do, right? (Yes!) And the child would likely get scolded by their parent, and told to say sorry, but we understand that toddlers are young and still learning, right? (Yes!)

Now think of yourself. What would happen if you pushed your classmate because they budged in line on the way to gym? (They might get held in for recess, sent to the behavior room, parent could be contacted, etc.)

It sounds like you'd get a harsher consequence than a 2-year-old. Why is that? (Because we know by now we shouldn't do that.)

And what about if I, an adult, pushed my co-worker because she was late to work and wasn't here to lead our Seeing Red *group? (Laugh.) I could lose my job or even get arrested, right?"*

Help the group understand that another important reason to work on their impulse control, and learn to control their behavior, is because as they get older, the consequences get more serious.

Seeing Red's Wood Block Statements

1. One way I show respect to others is by…

2. I've experienced being treated unfairly when…

3. When I get mad I usually want to….

4. Something I really want to change about my behavior sometimes is…

5. I feel really proud when I…

6. Something I really like about myself is…

7. My neighborhood feels _____ to me.

8. When I get mad I wish I…

9. Something that helps me when I am starting to feel angry is…

10. My family often shows their anger by…

11. Someone who helps me when my anger gets really big is…

12. It helps me to _____ when I'm angry.

13. A time recently when I said I was sorry was…

14. If there was less fighting I would feel…

15. I feel _____ about my school.

16. I feel _____ about my home.

17. Something I can do to be a positive leader is…

18. One thing adults can do to support kids is…

19. I wish adults understood _____ about me.

20. I am really good at…

List Of Resources

Books Related to Anger and Feeelings

Glad Monster, Sad Monster by Ed Emberley

My Many Colored Days by Dr. Suess

Alexander and the Terrible, Horrible, No Good, Very Bad Day by Judith Viorst

Today I Feel Silly: And Other Moods That Make My Day by Jamie Lee Curtis

Mad Isn't Bad: A Child's Book About Anger by Michaelene Mund

When Sophie Gets Angry—Really, Really Angry by Molly Bang

Soda Pop Head by Julia Cook

David Gets in Trouble by David Shannon

The Way I Feel by Janan Cain

Moody Cow Meditates by Kerry Lee MacLean

Angry Octopus: A Relaxation Story by Lori Lite

Books Related to Bullying and Bystanders

Llama Llama and the Bully Goat by Anna Dewdney

The Little Bit Scary People by Emily Jenkins

Just Kidding by Judy Trudwig

Sorry! by Trudy Ludwig

Say Something! by Peggy Moss

Simon's Hook: A Story About Teases and Put-downs by Karen Gedig Burnett

The Juice Box Bully: Empowering Kids to Stand Up for Others by Bob Somson

Enemy Pie by Derek Munson

Trouble Talk by Trudy Ludwig

Online Resources About Bullying and Cyerbullying

stopbullying.gov

stopcyberbullying.org

eyesonbullying.org

pacer.org/bullying

About the Author

JENNIFER SIMMONDS is Lead Program Coordinator at Fairview's Youth Grief Services, a program serving grieving children, teens and families. She holds a Masters of Education in Youth Development Leadership, and has facilitated hundreds of educational and support groups as well as workshops on peace-making, grief and loss, children in change, social skills and LGBT support. In addition to over two decades of experience facilitating small groups, Jennifer has served as adjunct faculty at the University of Minnesota in the Youth Studies Department and is also author of the popular resource *Children in Change*.

If you have enjoyed *Seeing Red*, you might also enjoy other

BOOKS TO BUILD A NEW SOCIETY

Our books provide positive solutions for people who want to
make a difference. We specialize in:

**Sustainable Living • Green Building • Peak Oil • Renewable Energy
Environment & Economy • Natural Building & Appropriate Technology
Progressive Leadership • Resistance and Community
Educational & Parenting Resources**

New Society Publishers

ENVIRONMENTAL BENEFITS STATEMENT

New Society Publishers has chosen to produce this book on recycled paper made with
100% post consumer waste, processed chlorine free, and old growth free.

For every 5,000 books printed, New Society saves the following resources:[1]

23	Trees
2,076	Pounds of Solid Waste
2,284	Gallons of Water
2,980	Kilowatt Hours of Electricity
3,774	Pounds of Greenhouse Gases
16	Pounds of HAPs, VOCs, and AOX Combined
6	Cubic Yards of Landfill Space

[1]Environmental benefits are calculated based on research done by the Environmental Defense Fund and
other members of the Paper Task Force who study the environmental impacts of the paper industry.

For a full list of NSP's titles, please call 1-800-567-6772 *or check out our website* at:

www.newsociety.com